Lee Bailey's
Southern Food
& Plantation Houses

Lee Bailey's Southern Food & Plantation Houses

Favorite Natchez Recipes

*by Lee Bailey
and the
Pilgrimage Garden Club*

Photographs by Tom Eckerle

Design by Hans Teensma

Clarkson N. Potter, Inc./Publishers

This book is dedicated to the memory
of that small band of purposeful ladies who began
the Natchez Pilgrimage almost a half century ago—
and to all the warm and generous people
of this lovely river city.

Endpaper design: "Cornwell's Journey" wallpaper from the Historic Natchez Collection by Schumacher.
Copyright © 1989. Used with permission.

Published by Clarkson N. Potter, Inc., 201 East 50th Street, New York,
New York 10022, and distributed by Crown Publishers, Inc.

CLARKSON N. POTTER, POTTER and colophon are trademarks of
Clarkson N. Potter, Inc.

Manufactured in Japan

Library of Congress Cataloging-in-Publication Data
Bailey, Lee.
Lee Bailey's southern food & plantation houses: Favorite Natchez recipes/by Lee Bailey and the Pilgrimage
Garden Club; photographs by Tom Eckerle.
p.   cm.
1. Cookery, American—Southern style.   2. Cookery—Mississippi—Natchez.   3. Plantations—Mississippi—
Natchez Region.   I. Pilgrimage Garden Club of Natchez.   II. Title.   III. Title: Lee Bailey's southern food
and plantation houses.   IV. Title: Southern food & plantation houses.
TX715.2.S68B35   1990
641.5975—dc20   89-16366
ISBN 0-517-58103-5

10 9 8 7 6 5 4 3 2 1

First Edition

Acknowledgments

FIRST, I'D LIKE TO EXPRESS MY APPRECIA-
tion to all of the owners of the splendid
houses in which we photographed, for not
only opening their houses and gardens
(and recipe files) to us, but also for their
genuine outpouring of hospitality and
cooperation.

In alphabetical order, at Banker's House,
Mr. and Mrs. Luther A. Stowers; at Chero-
kee, Mr. and Mrs. Hugh Junkin; at D'Eve-
reux, Mrs. Benny Buckles and Mr. and Mrs.
Jack Benson; at Dunleith, Mr. and Mrs.
William F. Heins III; at Edgewood, Mr. and
Mrs. Richard A. Campbell; at Elgin, Dr.
and Mrs. William F. Calhoun; at Green
Leaves, the Beltzhoover family; at Haw-
thorne, Mr. and Mrs. Hyde R. Jenkins; at
Hope Farm, Mrs. Ethel Green Banta; at
Lansdowne, Mr. and Mrs. John C. McIlroy,
Mr. and Mrs. Mackenzie Nobles; at Linden,
Mrs. J. Sanders Feltus; at Mistletoe, the
S. H. Lambdin Family Trust; at Monmouth,
Mr. and Mrs. Ron Riches; at Montaigne,
Mrs. Hunter Goodrich; at Oakland, Mr.
and Mrs. Lawrence Adams; at Routhland,
Mr. and Mrs. Charles E. Ratcliffe, Jr.;
at Stanton Hall, the Executive Commit-
tee of the Pilgrimage Garden Club; at
the Elms, Mrs. Alma Kellogg Carpenter;
at Twin Oaks, Dr. and Mrs. Homer
Whittington.

Also at Dunleith, Nancy Gibbs, Brenda
Smith, and Jackie Hargrave; at Elgin, Lizzie
Davis; at Monmouth, Margaret Burns; and
at Montaigne, Margaret McElinney.

Very special thanks to Courtney Parker,
who worked so diligently researching and
testing recipes with me—and as if that
wasn't enough, cooking all the food you
see here as well. You were terrific.

To Denise Gee, who did the historical
research and wrote the histories of the
houses. Many, many thanks.

To Sherry Jones, with an able assist from
Anna James, who kept us on schedule, saw
that we were housed and fed, and generally
did everything she could think of to help. It
wouldn't have been half so much fun without you.

And to Cindy Whittington and Alice
Feltus—flower ladies extraordinary. See a
close-up of their handiwork on pages 12
through 15.

For supplying extra accessories, thanks to
Dixon's Fine Gift, Buzz Harper, and Norma
Watson. And for helping us get the night
picture at Longwood, thanks to Mrs.
Anthony Burns and Marlon Copeland.

For my many good and helpful friends
at Clarkson N. Potter and Crown. As
usual, bravo! And to Pam Bernstein for
her support.

To Tom Eckerle, who did the photographs, assisted by Paul Sunday and Bill
Keese. Your work is more beautiful than
ever. As usual, it was a pleasure.

Finally to a new member of our team,
Hans Teensma, who designed this book.
A beautiful job!

And, of course, to my Natchez relatives,
the two Freddies, Dempse, Anne and
Leanne. With love.

CONTENTS

Introduction

NATCHEZ, MISSISSIPPI, BEING
home to my remarkable Aunt
Freddie and her family for so
many years, is naturally a place I have vis-
ited numerous times. And on almost every
trip I've been taken with just how good
the local food is, whether it be a Sunday
fried chicken dinner, a sprawling outdoor
barbecue, or a fish fry. It's not so much
that the place has a completely distinct
style of food, rather that it is so very rep-
resentative of the best Southern cooking.
After all, most of the South shares culi-
nary roots—but Natchez roots run deep.

And as if that weren't enough, when
you see the settings—that magnificent
classic nineteenth-century architecture in
the midst of tumbling flowers and towering trees—against which all this delectable
food is served, you can't help glimpsing,
for tantalizing moments, the glorious and
fertile past that originally spawned such
irresistible sensory treats. Such moments
make you feel as if a window somehow
magically had been opened into the past.

It was on a recent visit to Natchez that
I decided to start putting this book
together. Natchez food, it seems to me, is
essentially unassuming, based not on
sophisticated or complicated techniques
but on great natural abundance. When
you are blessed with what appears to be
an inexhaustible supply of ripening fruits

and vegetables, game, river fish, seafood
brought up from the Gulf, and more,
making good eating the focus of practically all occasions seems almost inevitable.

Not surprisingly, such food is still as
satisfying and warming now as it was on
those long-ago days when the houses and
their great trees were young.

So let's eat this wonderful food that has
evolved over almost two centuries—some
classic and some new—and let's eat it in
surroundings typical of those that produced these simple, but delectable, dishes
in the first place.

But before we get to the table and tie
on our bibs, a little background about
Natchez. If you're not a Southerner, it's
unlikely you would know that it is the oldest settlement on the Mississippi River, or
that it has a concentration of carefully
restored antebellum (pre–Civil War,
1861) houses greater than any other com-
parable place in the country—over five
hundred at latest count. An unverified
story is often repeated that just prior to
the Civil War there were more million-
aires living in and around here than in any
other American city outside of New York.
Well, real or apocryphal, with the great
nineteenth-century cotton boom and river

traffic then, it *could* be true. And anyway, the chronicle of such a lovely and historic place invites—almost demands—a bit of romantic hyperbole.

Directly across the muddy river waters, practically a mile wide at this point, are the flatlands of Louisiana, from whose sand and clay banks Natchez looks like a well-preserved time capsule of the last century. In many ways it is.

People hereabouts are proud to say that the local citizens have a reputation for being "inherently aristocratic." Family ties are unusually strong and historical preservation is a passion with many people. Consequently, more than 150,000 tourists visit the city each year. Some never leave.

Natchez was named after the Natchez Indians who lived in the area for hundreds of years before the white man ever showed up—and after he did, beginning with de Soto and his men in about 1542, things went pretty bad for them. At first it seems the Indians were curious and aloof, exhibiting the natural dignity that seemed to have characterized many early tribes' encounters with the first intruders. After all, the Indians were in some sense the hosts, having lived here for so many

Spring daffodils.

generations. And they were not, in the European sense, strictly territorial—believing all land and nature's plenitude was for their use, but not necessarily at the exclusion of others. However, the one thing they deemed unforgivable was the violation of their sacred grounds. And it was apparently the early settlers' continuing arrogant or stupid disregard of this taboo, beginning sometime around the 1720s, which led to a rupture between Indians and settlers and to the eventual extinction of the hapless Natchez.

As the village grew from a small French settlement to the bustling and thriving center of the plantation and river trade in the mid-nineteenth century, it passed from French to British to Spanish control before finally becoming a part of the newly formed Mississippi Territory in 1798.

Those citizens who prospered during Natchez's glory days were considered "aristocratic and intellectual," and as a matter of fact many held degrees from Eastern and European universities. Some were British nobility, younger sons who had missed out on inheriting family money and were forced to seek their fortune in the New World. Still others were Scottish, French, and Spanish—some polished, but all adventuresome. As the city thrived, there developed a tradition of lavish hospitality. There were cotillions, receptions, picnics, house parties, and barbecues. And of course at the center of all this activity was marvelous food.

Many celebrated people of the time journeyed to Natchez. Both Andrew Jackson and Jefferson Davis were married here and Aaron Burr, General Lafayette, Henry Clay, Jenny Lind, and Jim Bowie all enjoyed its graciousness on long visits. Even the notorious James brothers were said to have stopped over to sample the steamy pleasures that were available "Under-the-Hill"—the area where steamboats docked and ruffians amused themselves.

The burgeoning economy naturally had its effect on the architecture, and Federal and Greek revival styles became fashionable with many plantation owners. Greek revival, in particular, suited the newly wealthy gentlemen's desire to show off what their money and power could produce. Great soaring columns and Greek symmetry became a part of such palatial structures as Stanton Hall and D'Evereux. Older plantations like The Elms and

Hope Farm were renovated at this time, while the Georgian influence made itself felt in the restrained simplicity and sophistication of such houses as Lansdowne.

Architecture was at its most imposing just before 1861, as attested to by the disparate styles of houses like Dunleith and Longwood.

Then came the Civil War.

By the time Mississippi seceded from the Union, Natchez had a population of approximately 6,000 very wealthy people. Fortunately the city was able to escape the damage of war, unlike nearby Vicksburg. Of course, Union soldiers did set up camp in some of Natchez's finest houses, and many felt free to take home valuable souvenirs, although it is said that a sizable number of soldiers, being poor country lads, were too in awe of their surroundings to do much damage. Well whatever the true attitude of the occupying troops may have been, after the war ended Reconstruction unraveled Natchez's glory. Entrepreneurial carpetbaggers and angry freed slaves abused the city and its plantations, invading such glorious houses as Montaigne, for example. Later, few landowners had the money to pay Confederacy debt taxes, hire servants, or restore the vanished glory of their plantations. Many great houses either fell into ruin or became small colleges or boarding houses.

Savings were lost. Furnishings and jewelry were auctioned. Still, a few families, like the Marshalls at Lansdowne, the Bislands and Lambdins at Mistletoe, Mount Repose and Edgewood, among others, were able to fight successfully for the restoration of their fortunes.

But by 1932 Natchez was a dusty shadow of its past self. What the war had not done the Great Depression seemed about to accomplish. Then Hope Farm's

Katharine Grafton Miller, together with a group of like-minded genteel ladies, made a decision to try to rebuild and preserve their city. This determined group did what little work to their houses and gardens they could afford and sought to generate money to bolster the faltering local economy by opening their houses to paying visitors. The Tour, and the Natchez tourist industry, was born. Luckily their tradition of charming welcomes and good food had weathered the lean years and was once again ready to serve them.

Bearded iris.

As more and more people came to immerse themselves in the region's memories, money started trickling in and much-needed, but necessarily delayed, restorations were possible. The city was once again beginning to feel hopeful.

Then the trump card! Natchez's rich soil offered up OIL. Oil dollars produced a frenzy of restoration, building, and preservation until the beginning of the 1980s.

Now with the oil industry dozing, Natchez has once again returned to what has become its number one industry—its past. Today there are almost a hundred houses intermittently shown to tourists, and passenger paddle wheel steamboats like the *Delta* and *Mississippi Queen* once again dock at the Natchez Landing.

So if Natchez folk have anything to do with it, their city of tourists and history, good food and easy living will always be, as one Natchez matriarch plainly put it, "where the Old South still lives."

Amen.

Natchez Bouquets

ONE OF THE BONUSES OF BEING in Natchez for the time it took to do the photographs and write the text for this book was becoming reacquainted with the flowers and plants of my childhood.

TOP: **Pink Perfection camellias.** ABOVE: **Coreopsis, kalanchoe flower, and foliage.**

Of course I remembered perfectly most of the shrubs, trees, and flowers I saw, but their names seemed to escape me. For instance, there is a bush that has sprays of small leaves on individual stems growing out, umbrella fashion, from its main trunk. In late spring, little cream-colored flowers appear on the crown of this bush, and after they are finished, red berries. It's not so much that this bush was one of my favorites, because it wasn't; it's just that the plant was so familiar and I couldn't

for the life of me recall its name. Not being able to remember almost drove me bonkers before I finally got it: nandina.

In reality, it practically became a point of honor with me to dredge up these names without having to ask. Do you think maybe I was being a little obsessive?

Fortunately, there are a couple of local ladies who not only know the names of all the flowers hereabouts but who know what to do with them: Cindy Whittington and Alice Feltus. Together and separately, they made almost all the bouquets in the rooms you see here, searching out flowers everywhere. While they were at it, they more than a few times came up with marvelous little bouquets that called out to be photographed—just because they were so lovely. So here they are, Cindy and Alice's beautiful small bouquets.

Spirea, cherry laurel, Lady Banksia rose, wild onion, and
two varieties of tazetta narcissus.

Muscari (Grape Hyacinth), pansies, and
Confederate jasmine.

Wild clematis and summer roses.

Summer roses.

Wild ageratum and lantana.

Torenia, blooming basil,
chrysanthemum, and wild ageratum.

Asclepias, bougainvillea,
ageratum, and cosmos.

Blue and white torenia, begonia,
wild ageratum, and melampodium.

Informal Dinner at Stanton Hall

STANTON HALL STANDS TODAY IN testament to the wealth and vitality of antebellum Natchez. Yet the elegant three-story mansion was not enjoyed long by its builder, Frederick Stanton (1794–1859). A cotton broker whose considerable wealth flowed from hugely successful plantations in both Mississippi and Louisiana, Stanton died only months after moving into his grand new house. For its setting he had purchased an entire block of downtown Natchez and hired architect Thomas Rose; later Stanton sent Rose to Europe to bring back suitably splendid furnishings and custom-made architectural detailing.

Stanton Hall's interior encompasses a spacious basement, wine cellar, two floors of living quarters, a billiard room, card room, and a music room with an observation room crowning its roof. Surrounding the Greek revival house was an iron fence, enclosing many live oaks and a multitude of azaleas. All told more than $83,000 was spent to enhance the main building's glory, an amount that mystified early Natchez citizens.

Requiring more than eight years to build and first named "Belfast," it was finished in 1858. To complete the compound, next to the main building, a three-story servants' wing and a carriage house were added. All these structures were made from native clay brick—fired, stuccoed, and painted white on the property

during Belfast's construction. Local craftsmen were contracted to add to Belfast's furnishings. A 35-foot dining room table, still used where it was originally placed, is one of those pieces.

After Stanton's death, his wife, Hulda Helm Stanton, and her large family remained in residence until her death in 1893. The house survived the Civil War intact, with only scarred pillars from Union gunboats, and Union troops were billeted in the servants' quarters.

Belfast changed hands several times, first becoming Stanton College for Young Ladies—the destiny for a number of grand houses after the Civil War. Then for a decade beginning in 1903, Stanton Hall, as it was by then named, was occupied by Stanton descendants, Mr. and Mrs. A. G. Campbell.

During the 1930s, the house was owned by the R. T. Clark family. Finally, in 1938, the Pilgrimage Garden Club bought the property, furnished it with the Stanton family pieces that could be found, and now uses the well-preserved buildings as their headquarters. The club is dedicated to the preservation of just such glorious structures, which seems only fitting.

Stanton Hall has been a museum and a National Historic Landmark listed in the National Register of Historic Places. It has been the headquarters of the Pilgrimage Garden Club since 1938.

Denise Gee

MENU

Tomato Aspic with Mayonnaise

Spicy Milk Fried Chicken with Pan Gravy

Pecan Rice

Spring Peas and Green Onions

Biscuits

Baked Custard with Adelina Patti Grape Dessert Sauce

Iced Tea or Wine · Coffee

THE MEAL IN THEIR PRESENT INCARnation, the servants' quarters and the carriage house that are part of the Stanton Hall grounds have been turned into a restaurant, which is as popular with the local population as it is with visitors—proof (if any were needed) of the quality and kind of food served there. Its most enduring menu is a classic in every way, so we figured there was no point in tampering with success.

With the agreement of Dorothy Clark, the manager and sometimes chief-cook at the restaurant, we added toasted pecans to the rice, as is often done in the homes here, and we came up with a grape dessert sauce to top the baked custard, naming it

PRECEDING PAGE, LEFT:
**Glorious spring
flowers in the drawing
room.** PRECEDING PAGE, RIGHT:
Stanton Hall. ABOVE:
**Corinthian-inspired
capital.** OPPOSITE: **Dinner
in the library.**

in honor of the lady in a pink dress whose portrait hangs over one of the sideboards in the large dining room of the main houses.

Otherwise, the menu was typical of ones that have been served ever since fried chicken became synonymous with good Southern country living. In this case we decided to serve it in the library, which was probably originally used on occasion for informal dinners.

I was told that the "secret" of this delicious fried chicken is that it is soaked in seasoned milk before being fried. Whatever, it's no secret that this fried chicken was about as good as it gets, and the pan gravy was just right.

The meal began with tomato aspic. I don't know when this dish first gained popularity in these parts, but in many local restaurants aspic is as ubiquitous as iced tea. I do know it's something I grew up with and still like. It's only too bad that many people equate tomato aspic with tearooms and ladies' luncheons. But I say, so what! It's still good. Pot pies suffered the same fate—and look where they are today.

The vegetable was green peas combined with green onions—another staple. And, of course, how could you have fried chicken without biscuits?

TOMATO ASPIC with MAYONNAISE

When this was made at home, our cook prepared extra to serve with sandwiches and the like. The recipe also will give you extras.

- ½ cup boiling water
- 2 envelopes unflavored gelatin
- 3 cups thick tomato juice, warmed
- 1 small onion, very finely minced
- 2 ribs celery, very finely minced
- 1 tablespoon freshly squeezed lemon juice
- 2 teaspoons Worcestershire sauce
- 1 teaspoon salt
- ½ teaspoon freshly ground black pepper
- ½ teaspoon Tabasco
- 8 ounces cream cheese

Pour the hot water into a shallow bowl and sprinkle gelatin over it. When gelatin is completely dissolved, stir in the warmed tomato juice, making sure all lumps are gone; if they persist, reheat the mixture briefly. Stir in all other ingredients except cream cheese and cool slightly. Meanwhile, divide the cream cheese by spoonfuls among twelve ½-cup molds. Pour tomato mixture in each and refrigerate until set, several hours.

To serve, run a knife around the top of each mold and set in a bowl of hot water just long enough to loosen gelatin. Place a serving plate on top and invert to unmold. If water has melted the aspic too much, rerefrigerate long enough to set again. Put a dab of homemade mayonnaise on each and garnish with a sprig of green, if you like.

Makes 12

SPRING PEAS AND GREEN ONIONS

If you are not a green-onion fancier, omit them and simply serve the peas buttered.

- 1 tablespoon unsalted butter, or more to taste
- 1 large bunch green onions, coarsely chopped, including some top
- 3 cups fresh or frozen green peas
- ½ teaspoon salt, or more to taste
- ½ cup water

Melt the butter in a medium saucepan and add the green onions. Sauté about 5 minutes, until just wilted, being careful not to let them brown. Add the peas and sprinkle with salt. Add water and cover tightly. Simmer for about 10 minutes or more, until peas are tender. Timing will depend on age and size of the peas and if they are fresh or frozen. Frozen peas take only a few minutes. If, when the peas are almost tender, there is too much liquid, uncover, turn the heat up to high, and quickly boil some out. Serve immediately.

Serves 6

BELOW: **Federal-style glass front bookcase in the library of Stanton Hall.** ABOVE: **Tomato Aspic with Mayonnaise.** OPPOSITE: **Porcelain shepherdess among the camellias.**

PECAN RICE

No matter how I use pecans, I almost always toast them first, except when I am making a pecan pie. I find toasting vastly improves their flavor, as it does most nuts.

1 **cup pecans**

1 **tablespoon unsalted butter**

3 **cups hot cooked long-grain rice (not instant), rinsed well**
   Salt and freshly ground black pepper (optional)

Preheat the oven to 250 degrees. Place the pecans in a single layer on a baking sheet and toast about 15 minutes, until golden but not burned. Chop coarsely and set aside.

When ready to serve, melt the butter in a skillet and add pecans, stirring to coat with butter. Add the rice and toss with pecans. Add a grind of fresh pepper and more salt, if you like.

Serves 6

ABOVE: **Cozy corner in an upstairs bedroom.** BELOW: **Detail of Earl Hart Miller needlepoint rug in the library.** RIGHT: **Spring Peas and Green Onions, Pan Gravy, and Pecan Rice.**

SPICY MILK FRIED CHICKEN with PAN GRAVY

I understand that the Louisiana hot sauce used in the marinade is regularly available in stores throughout the country. It is not as hot as the fiery Tabasco, although surely no slouch in the heat department.

- 4 **cups milk**
- 1 **cup Louisiana hot sauce**
- 3 **tablespoons salt**
- 1 **pound all-purpose flour**
- 2 **medium frying chickens, cut into small serving pieces**
  Oil for frying
- 1 **cup chicken stock, approximately**
  Freshly ground black pepper

Mix the milk and hot sauce in a small pitcher and stir in about 1 tablespoon of the salt. Place the chicken pieces in a shallow pan and pour with mixture over. Turn once and marinate for 30 minutes. Meanwhile, put half the flour and remaining salt in a brown paper bag and tear off several large sheets of waxed paper. Place the paper conveniently on the counter next to the stove. Lift the chicken out of the milk mixture and allow to drain slightly before putting in the flour bag. Do this in batches. Shake chicken to coat well. Lift out, shake off excess flour, and place on the waxed paper. Repeat until all the chicken is coated, using more salted flour as necessary.

Pour at least 2 inches of vegetable oil in a deep skillet. Heat to 300 degrees (I use a candy thermometer but a thermostat-controlled deep-fat fryer, such as a Fry Daddy, is also a good idea.) Put chicken in, but do not crowd. Fry, adjusting the heat to keep flour from burning, 15 minutes, turning a couple of times. Place on a cooling rack to drain, underneath which you have placed double sheets of paper towels. Keep an eye on the skillet so flour does not burn, and continue until all the chicken is cooked. You may want to do this in 2 large skillets.

To make pan gravy, carefully pour off all the oil from the browned flour and chicken bits left in the pan. Add the chicken stock and simmer a few minutes, until thickened. Adjust seasoning with salt and a generous amount of black pepper.

Serves 6

TOP: **Spicy Milk Fried Chicken.** ABOVE: **Mantel detail from the library.**

BISCUITS

If by some miracle you have any of these left over, they are awfully good at breakfast, split, buttered, toasted under the broiler, and spread with jam.

- 2 cups all-purpose flour
- 4 teaspoons baking powder
- ¼ teaspoon salt
- 1 teaspoon sugar
- 5 tablespoons solid vegetable shortening, chilled
- ¾ to 1 cup cold milk, plus additional for tops

Preheat the oven to 450 degrees. Place all the dry ingredients in a food processor and give it a few whirls to mix. Add shortening and process, turning off and on a few times, until mixture is the texture of coarse meal. (You may also cut in the shortening with a pastry cutter or 2 knives if you don't have a food processor.) Pour in milk through the feed tube with the motor running, until mixture forms a ball. Stop immediately and roll dough out on a floured surface with a floured rolling pin to a thickness of about ¼ inch. Cut into 2-inch biscuits. Gather up the scraps and form into a ball, flatten, and cut more biscuits until all dough is used.

Place on ungreased baking sheets and paint tops with milk, if you like, to make them brown more. Bake for 15 minutes or until golden brown.

These are usually split and buttered in the kitchen while they are still very hot. (If you don't serve them right away, keep in a warm oven.)

Makes 36

TOP: **Biscuits.** ABOVE LEFT: **Etched glass coal oil lamp in the drawing room.** ABOVE RIGHT: **An upstairs bedroom.**

BAKED CUSTARD
with ADELINA PATTI GRAPE DESSERT SAUCE

A long, slow baking time is called for here—the results are worth it. The sauce is named for the pink in A. P.'s dress.

- 3 large eggs
- ⅓ cup sugar
- ½ teaspoon vanilla extract
  Dash of salt
- 2 cups milk
  Adelina Patti Grape Dessert Sauce (recipe follows)
  Whipped cream (optional)

Preheat the oven to 275 degrees. To make custard, beat eggs lightly, then add the sugar and continue to beat until sugar begins to dissolve. Stir in the vanilla and salt. Carefully stir in the milk, mixing well. Pour into 6 individual ½-cup molds and place in a roasting pan. Surround with boiling water about three-fourths up the sides. Bake for 20 minutes. Turn back heat to 250 degrees and bake for another hour and 40 minutes, or until a knife inserted into the custard comes out clean. Remove molds from water and allow to cool. Serve with dessert sauce and whipped cream, if desired.

Serves 6

ADELINA PATTI GRAPE DESSERT SAUCE

- 6 tablespoons sugar
- 6 tablespoons freshly squeezed lemon juice
- 3 cups red seedless grapes, halved

Mix sugar and lemon juice in a skillet over medium to low heat, stirring until sugar begins to dissolve, about 2 minutes. Turn heat to medium and add grapes, tossing. Cook over high heat for about 8 minutes. Off the heat, remove grapes with a slotted spoon, then return skillet to heat. Simmer over medium to high heat for a few minutes until juice begins to thicken. Add grapes and allow to cool.

Makes about 3 cups

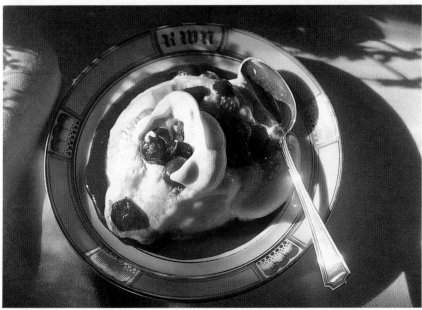

TOP: **Rococo revival chair in the drawing room, circa 1850.** ABOVE: **Baked Custard with Adelina Patti Grape Dessert Sauce.**

Elgin Barbecue

ELGIN PLANTATION SITS SNUG beneath moss-hung live oak, pecan, and magnolia trees, overlooking twenty-five acres of orchards and gardens.

A young doctor from Pennsylvania, John Carmichael Jenkins, and his new wife, Annis Dunbar, settled in the Natchez countryside, where Annis's family owned the Forest Plantation. Jenkins bought the sister cottage and property to the plantation in 1840 and set about refurbishing the old house. He renamed it Elgin as a tribute to the birthplace of

Annis's Scotch grandfather.

To accommodate both Southern hospitality and his future family, Jenkins set forth to further expand his home, never intending it to be a showplace. By 1855, most of the work was completed, and Jenkins had built wings of rooms to the north and south of Elgin. In 1852, the Forest Plantation burned, leaving behind some 16,000 bricks for Jenkins to use for a servants' quarters and kitchen outbuilding.

The dependency, now used for guests, was unique for its giant order columns,

presumably from the Forest, that added a touch of elegance to a building otherwise built for simplicity.

Detailed journals kept by Dr. Jenkins, combined with letters mentioning the home, show that the plantation atmosphere was rich in food and celebration. Champagne flowed, and figs, strawberries, cakes, and jellies were consumed in abundance, as were venison, pork, and poultry.

When Elgin's restructuring was completed, the Jenkins family numbered four. The house was, as it is today, broad but shallow, with five rooms across and only one room deep.

Outside in Elgin's orchard today, there are fruit trees that were once seedlings planted by Jenkins. A few of the original boxwood and camellia bushes remain in the formal garden, as do some cedars.

Not far away is the Jenkins family cemetery, a haven of English ivy and magnolias. Along with other family members, Dr. and Mrs. Jenkins are buried there, having died from an epidemic of yellow fever in 1855. Supposedly, the large live oak tree that commands the middle of the cemetery marks Dr. Jenkins's grave.

It seems fitting that another doctor, William F. Calhoun, and his wife, Ruth Ellen, purchased the by-then deserted house in 1975 and have restored Elgin to its original charm.

Elgin and its grounds have been open to tourists intermittently since 1932. The house is listed in the National Register of Historic Places.

D. G.

PRECEDING PAGE, ABOVE: **The winding drive leading to Elgin.** PRECEDING PAGE, BELOW: **Elgin Plantation.** ABOVE: **Side stairs leading to the front gallery.** BELOW: **Old-fashioned camellia.** RIGHT: **Looking out toward the orchard.** FAR RIGHT: **The dining room set for dinner.** OPPOSITE: **Hardy azalea.**

M E N U

Natchez Sloe Gin Rickey

Slow Oven-Barbecued Brisket

Black-Eyed Pea Salad with Champagne Vinaigrette

Baked Honey Tomatoes

Skillet Fresh Corn

Cheese-Stuffed French Loaf

Strawberries with Brown Sugar and Sour Cream

Wine · Coffee

THE MEAL ELGIN PLANTATION rests comfortably in a neat but unmanicured landscape full of ancient trees and blooming shrubs. The house itself, which is even rustic in some parts, has a welcoming openness enhanced by its long front gallery. This combination of place, space, and style somehow seemed to invite a meal that would be both hearty and simple—one as satisfyingly direct as its setting, its elegant past and occupants notwithstanding.

The before-dinner drink was a reminder of the twenties, but the barbecued beef was certainly something that would have been served when Elgin was built in the nineteenth century—only it probably would have been cooked in an outdoor open pit in those days. Here we chose to do brisket baked in the oven. The recipe calls for soy sauce—which would have been pretty hard to come by back then unless a bottle could have somehow found its way south from one of the kitchens of the Oriental workmen helping to open the West—but it's true in spirit. And the slow oven cooking makes this "barbecued" brisket moist and flavorful, well able to hold its own with its pit-roasted relative.

We also tinkered with another staple—black-eyed peas—and made a salad dressed with a sweet Champagne vinaigrette.

The other accompaniments were creamy skillet corn and honeyed tomatoes, both prepared pretty much as they have been hereabouts for ages. Finally, the bread was made special with a stuffing of cheese and onions.

After all this, we figured a big bowl of ripe strawberries with brown sugar and sour cream would be just the right finish.

NATCHEZ SLOE
GIN RICKEY

If sloe gin is not to your liking substitute either regular dry gin or vodka. And the amount of sparkling water, lemon juice, cassis, and sugar are all variable according to personal taste.

8 fluid ounces (1 cup) sloe gin, or more to taste

Juice of 4 large lemons

Simple Syrup (see Note)

30 fluid ounces (about 2¾ cups) sparkling water

Cassis (black currant liqueur)

Lemon slices and mint sprigs (optional)

Mix the gin, lemon juice, and simple syrup, if you are using it, in a small pitcher. Fill with cracked ice and stir in sparkling water. Stir a few more times and pour into 6 ice-filled glasses. Give each a dash of cassis and garnish with lemon and mint sprigs.

Makes 6 drinks

NOTE: To make simple syrup combine 1 part water with 2 parts sugar Slowly boil for 5 minutes. Cool be fore using.

BELOW: **Unusual double rocker on the porch.**
RIGHT: **Natchez Sloe Gin Rickeys and pecans for nibbling on the veranda.**

SLOW OVEN-BARBECUED BRISKET

This is a meat dish that reheats very well. Unlike some cuts of beef which are best when rare or pink, brisket is best when thoroughly cooked, so overcooking is not a problem when this dish is reheated. However, don't let the brisket dry out, for moistness is one of this method of cooking's most appealing qualities.

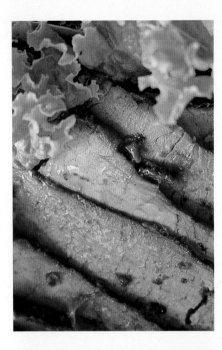

LEFT: **Slow Oven-Barbecued Brisket.** BELOW: **Looking down into the entrance hall.**

- 7- to 9-pound first cut beef brisket
- 1 generous teaspoon minced garlic
- 1 teaspoon celery seeds
- 3 tablespoons freshly ground black pepper
- 1 teaspoon ground ginger (optional)
- 4 large bay leaves, crumbled
- 1 (12-ounce) can tomato paste
- 1 cup dark soy sauce
- ½ cup Worcestershire sauce
- 1 cup tightly packed dark brown sugar
- 2 medium onions, thinly sliced

Preheat the oven to 350 degrees. Tear off 2 large pieces of foil, enough to completely enclose and seal in the brisket. Place the meat on the double sheets of foil and rub it on all sides with the garlic.

Combine the celery seeds, pepper, ginger, and crushed bay leaf, then sprinkle on all sides. Mix the tomato paste, soy sauce, Worcestershire sauce, and brown sugar, and smear this on the meat.

Score the fat side of the brisket and place the onions on top. Wrap in the foil and carefully seal by folding it down well. Place fat side up on a rack in a roasting pan. Cook in the foil for 4 hours.

Open the foil to expose the onion-covered top and cook for another hour.

Remove meat to a heated plate and keep warm. Meanwhile, degrease the sauce, add a bit of water, beer, or wine, if you like, then reduce. To serve, slice thinly against the grain and top with a spoon of sauce. Pass balance of the sauce.

Serves 8, with leftovers

BAKED HONEY TOMATOES

A lot of people don't realize how well the flavors of tomato and honey go together. These are easy, and once cooked may even wait if your timing of some other part of the meal is slightly off.

- 8 ripe medium tomatoes
- ½ cup fresh coarse bread crumbs
- 2 teaspoons salt
- 2 teaspoons freshly ground black pepper
- 1 tablespoon dried tarragon
- 4 teaspoons honey
- 4 teaspoons unsalted butter

Preheat the oven to 350 degrees. Slice off the stem ends of the tomatoes and carefully scoop out the seeds. Place open side up in a buttered baking dish.

Mix the bread crumbs with the salt, pepper, and tarragon. Drizzle the honey over the tomatoes, rubbing it down into the cavities. Sprinkle tomatoes with the crumb mixture and dot with butter. Bake, uncovered, for 30 minutes, until the tomato skins begin to wrinkle. Place under the broiler for another 5 minutes, or until crumbs begin to brown.

Serve hot or at room temperature.

Serves 8

BLACK-EYED PEA SALAD with CHAMPAGNE VINAIGRETTE

If you have to make this salad far enough in advance for it to require refrigeration, be sure to allow time for it to come to room temperature before serving. This can take up to an hour.

8 cups water

1 tablespoon plus 1 teaspoon salt

3 tablespoons dried basil

3 pounds frozen black-eyed peas

2 medium sweet red peppers, cut into medium dice

2 medium bell peppers, cut into medium dice

1 large red onion, thinly sliced

⅓ cup sweet Champagne, such as Asti Spumante

⅓ cup rice wine vinegar

⅔ cup safflower oil

1 teaspoon freshly ground black pepper

Combine the water, 1 tablespoon salt, and basil in a large saucepan. Bring to a boil and simmer for 5 minutes. Add the peas and cook over medium heat for about 45 minutes, until peas are tender but not musy. Drain and allow to cool.

Toss in the peppers and onion.

Whisk together the Champagne, vinegar, oil, remaining teaspoon salt, and pepper. Pour over the peas and marinate for several hours. Serve at room temperature.

Serves 8 or more

TOP: **Black-Eyed Pea Salad with Champagne Vinaigrette.**
ABOVE: **Baked Honey Tomatoes.**
ABOVE RIGHT: **Pear blossoms.**

SKILLET FRESH CORN

*Evaporated skim milk can be substi-
tuted for the half-and-half. And if the
corn is past its prime, a dash of sugar
will help.*

2 tablespoons unsalted butter
3 cups fresh corn kernels cut
  from the cob, about 12 ears
  (see Note)
½ cup half-and-half
1 teaspoon salt
½ teaspoon freshly ground black
  pepper

Melt the butter in a large skillet.
When it begins to bubble, add the
corn and mix. Stir in half-and-half,
salt, and pepper. Sauté over medium
heat, for 6 minutes, just long enough
to heat thoroughly and cook corn.

Serves 8

NOTE: When corn is cut from the
cob, be sure to scrape out the juice
from the cob with the dull side of the
knife and add to kernels.

CHEESE-STUFFED FRENCH LOAF

*If your time or patience has run out
by the time you get to this bread, you
might certainly serve plain French
bread heated.*

1 large loaf French bread
¾ cup (1½ sticks) unsalted
  butter, softened
1 teaspoon dried thyme
½ teaspoon Tabasco
½ cup sliced red onions
2 cups grated sharp cheddar
  cheese

Preheat the oven to 400 degrees. Cut
the bread lengthwise. Beat the butter
with the thyme and Tabasco, and
spread mixture on both insides of the
loaf. Lay the onions on the bottom
slice and sprinkle evenly with cheese.
Top with the other slice and wrap
securely with foil. Bake for about 20
to 25 minutes or until crust is hard.
Slice crosswise to serve.

Serves 8

TOP: **Skillet Fresh Corn.**
ABOVE: **Cheese-Stuffed
Loaf.** RIGHT: **Pear tree.**

STRAWBERRIES with BROWN SUGAR AND SOUR CREAM

This combination also works well with freshly sliced, peeled peaches. But it's best to toss them with a bit of lemon juice to keep discoloration to a minimum if you make this substitution. Serve the peaches with a spoon.

2 pints large strawberries, washed

1 cup dark brown sugar, firmly packed

1 pint sour cream

Place berries, brown sugar, and sour cream in separate bowls and allow guests to help themselves, first to the strawberries, then the toppings of sour cream and brown sugar.

Serves 8

TOP: **Strawberries with Brown Sugar and Sour Cream.**
ABOVE: **Punka fan over the dining room.**

Old-Fashioned Dinner at Hawthorne

HAWTHORNE WAS THE SCENE of many social gatherings, most notably a lavish reception hosted for the French general Lafayette in 1825. But unlike other antebellum Natchez houses, whose histories are well documented, Hawthorne's is decidedly hazy.

A typical planter's house, modestly elegant on the exterior yet spacious inside, Hawthorne is believed to have been built for Jonathan Thompson.

Thompson married Anna Williams of Gloucester Plantation, stepdaughter of Mississippi's first territorial governor. It seems likely that the Thompsons built their house in 1814, not far from Gloucester. What is known for certain is that tragedy befell the family in 1825, when both Thompsons were carried off by yellow fever. Hawthorne was probably next owned by George Overaker. Some contend that Overaker, and not the Thompsons, actually built Hawthorne, but this has not been authenticated.

Whatever the case, shortly after acquiring Hawthorne, Overaker gave it to one of his daughters, who later traded it for *her* sister's house. Thereafter, Hawthorne changed hands several times. Its most notable, well-documented owner was Robert Dunbar, of a Scottish clan. But, like the Thompsons, the Dunbar family also met with misfortune: Robert Dunbar died in the Civil War, and within months his children died of yellow fever.

The one-and-a-half-story house stands almost as it did then—shielded by lush greenery but offering a splendid view from its gallery. At Hawthorne's entrance, handsomely paneled double front doors open below a sunburst fanlight, a design unique to Natchez. There are four such elliptical architectural elements in the entrance hall of the house, all lighted from within by rows of candles.

The hand-hewn stairwell is tucked away from the main hallway to give the entrance a more open quality. Hawthorne's construction is of particular interest because of its plasterized brick nogging, found in medieval English and some early American structures.

Outside, the remains of an original barn, carriage house, brick kitchen, and even a plasterized privy can still be seen.

The house is presently owned by Bettye and Hyde Dunbar Jenkins. Although Hyde Jenkins is a descendant of both the Dunbar and the Jenkins families of Elgin and the Forest Plantations, Hawthorne was actually given to the couple in 1959 by Mrs. Jenkins' mother, Mrs. Randolph Pipes, who had lived there since 1937.

Hawthorne has been a point of interest for tourists visiting Natchez for more than fifty years, and it is listed in the National Register of Historic Places.

D. G.

Spring Sausage with Sautéed Onions

Mustard Greens with Pepper Vinegar

Buttered Rice and Mushrooms

Skillet Corn Bread

Bourbon-Mint Ice Cream

Sugar Cookies

Iced Tea or Wine · Coffee

THE MEAL HAWTHORNE HAS A lovely, large dining room that you see just as you come into the house, a room not tucked away inconspicuously behind the library or music room as it often is in other such houses. So you know right off that this is a place where food has always been an important part of entertaining.

The informality and generously inviting quality of this dining room seemed to call for an old-fashioned dinner, so we asked around to find out what everyone's favorite country food was. Here you have the menu we came up with from our extremely unscientific research.

As you see, the dinner included spring sausage with sautéed onions. Actually, the sausage was about neck-and-neck with baked chicken in our little poll, but since we were having chicken elsewhere, we settled on the sausage.

However, the mustard greens, buttered rice (or rice and gravy), and corn bread were agreed upon unanimously. And the ice cream and cookies were a pretty popular choice, too.

But the story doesn't end there. As we usually did when we were going to photograph in a house in which we hadn't cooked before, we tried to prepare most of the food in advance in a familiar kitchen. That way we were free to take advantage of the light as it shifted around the rooms. Obviously, unfamiliar kitchens can make for unwanted delays. So when we got to Hawthorne on the morning of the shoot we hadn't actually told Mr. and Mrs. Jenkins what menu we had decided upon. And since they were both busy, it wasn't until noon that we got around to discussing it with them. I remarked that the mustard greens we had brought along were smelling mighty good. Well, as it turns out the good smells were actually coming from Hawthorne's own kitchen, for the Jenkins' cook, Ernestine Williams, was cooking mustard greens for lunch! As a matter of fact, the Jenkins were having exactly the same meal (with chicken instead of sausage) as the menu we had planned for the house. So I guess we were right on the button with this one.

PRECEDING PAGE, LEFT: **Rockers on the veranda.** PRECEDING PAGE, RIGHT: **Hawthorne Plantation.** ABOVE: **Pink Perfection camellia.**

SPRING SAUSAGE
with SAUTÉED
ONIONS

It is important to make this enough in advance so that the flavors can mature. Pinch off a small piece of sausage and fry it to check the seasoning before doing the whole batch.

- 2 pounds ground pork
- 1 pound pork fat
- ¼ teaspoon cayenne pepper
- ¼ teaspoon coarsely ground black pepper
- ⅛ teaspoon dried sage
- ⅛ teaspoon dried thyme
- ⅛ teaspoon ground allspice
- ¼ teaspoon mace
- 1 teaspoon dark brown sugar
- 1½ tablespoons salt
- 1 clove garlic, minced
- ¼ cup minced onions
- ¼ cup chopped pecans
- 2 tablespoons Grand Marnier (optional)
  Sautéed Onions (recipe follows)

Place meat and fat in a bowl and sprinkle with sausage ingredients. Mix well by hand, lifting, not mashing; if you overwork this it will pack and become tough.

Wrap well and refrigerate for 12 to 24 hours to allow flavors to marry.

Form into patties. Place in a cold skillet and fry about 10 minutes, until browned on both sides and done in middle. Serve with Sautéed Onions.

Makes 13 medium patties

SAUTÉED ONIONS

Vidalia onions are available in most grocery stores in season.

- 4 tablespoons (½ stick) unsalted butter
- 4 large Vidalia onions, sliced or chopped coarsely

Melt butter over low heat and add onions, coating well. Cook about 8 minutes, until transparent and soft. Increase heat to caramelize sugar in onions, about 5 minutes. Stir constantly.

Remove onions from skillet, then use same skillet to cook mushrooms for the Buttered Rice (see page 41).

Serves 6 to 8

TOP: **Spring Sausage with Sautéed Onions, Mustard Greens, and Buttered Rice and Mushrooms.** ABOVE: **Child's chair.**

MUSTARD GREENS
with PEPPER VINEGAR

I've found that mustard greens are among the few vegetables that freeze well. They are so sturdy that the process doesn't ruin their texture.

- 6 **bunches mustard greens**
  Salt
- 4 **or 5 slices salt-cured hog jowls or thick bacon**
- 1 **large clove garlic, minced**
- 1 **teaspoon sugar**
  Freshly ground black pepper
  Pepper vinegar (see Note)

Wash the greens by stripping the leaves from the stems (discard stems) and placing them in a sink filled with cold water. Sprinkle a tablespoon of salt over them and swish around. Allow sediment to settle and lift out greens, shaking off excess water, but not drying.

In a heavy pot over medium-low heat, fry pork until just translucent and curled, about 5 minutes. Add garlic, being careful not to burn. Add wet greens and sugar, and cover. Stir and lift greens as they wilt in cooking.

Cook 1 hour or until tender.

Taste the pot liquor and add salt and pepper if necessary. Allow to drain slightly as greens are served. Sprinkle with pepper vinegar.

Serves 6 to 8

NOTE: Pepper vinegar is made most places by pouring about one-fourth of the vinegar out of a cider-vinegar bottle and then filling it with hot peppers. The peppers are marinated for several days.

BUTTERED RICE AND MUSHROOMS

You could substitute rice boiled in chicken stock and then butter it if you like.

- 2 tablespoons unsalted butter
- 2 cups sliced fresh mushrooms
- 4 cups cooked long-grain rice (not instant)

  Salt and freshly ground black pepper

Melt the butter in "onion skillet" (see page 39) and sauté the mushrooms over medium heat for a few minutes until they give up liquid. Sauté another 2 minutes and toss with the rice. Add more butter and salt and pepper to taste.

Serves 6 to 8

SKILLET CORN BREAD

The important thing for this recipe is to have the skillet as hot as you can get it.

- 1 cup yellow cornmeal
- 1 cup all-purpose flour
- ½ teaspoon sugar (optional)
- 4 teaspoons baking powder
- ½ teaspoon salt
- ¼ cup safflower oil or bacon drippings
- 1 egg
- 1½ cups milk, approximately

Place a large cast-iron skillet in the oven and turn temperature to 400 degrees. While the oven and the pan are preheating, mix dry ingredients in a bowl. Mix oil, egg, and milk, then stir into dry ingredients. Add a bit more milk if batter is stiff.

Remove skillet from the oven. Grease quickly with vegetable oil or bacon fat and pour the batter in, smoothing with a spatula if necessary. Bake about 20 minutes, until golden brown.

Serve hot from the skillet.

Serve 6 to 8

BOURBON-MINT
ICE CREAM

I love the taste of bourbon in desserts. It is especially good for flavoring whipped cream.

- 2 cups milk
- ¼ cup bourbon
- 2 tablespoons chopped fresh mint
- 3 eggs
- 1 cup sugar
- ½ teaspoon salt
- 1½ cups heavy cream
- 1½ teaspoons vanilla extract

Place milk, bourbon, and mint in a saucepan and bring just to a boil over low heat. Meanwhile, beat eggs and sugar until lemon yellow. Pour in a little hot milk to heat it, then pour egg mixture into warm milk, stirring all the while. Return to low heat (or transfer to a double boiler), and cook, stirring constantly, for 10 minutes, or until mixture coats a spoon. Strain and cool, then refrigerate. Stir in cream and vanilla, and pour mixture into a commercial ice-cream maker. Freeze in an ice-cream freezer according to manufacturer's instructions.

Makes 1 quart

LEFT: **Milk glass containers in the bedroom.** BELOW: **Quilted coverlet detail.** BOTTOM: **Bourbon-Mint Ice Cream and Sugar Cookies.**

SUGAR COOKIES

These have a flavor that complements ice cream very nicely. And they keep well.

- 2½ cups all-purpose flour
- 1½ teaspoons baking powder
- ½ teaspoon salt
- ¼ teaspoon ground cinnamon
- ¼ teaspoon grated nutmeg
- 1 cup sugar, plus extra for coating
- ¾ cup safflower oil
- 2 eggs
- 1 teaspoon vanilla extract

Preheat the oven to 375 degrees. Sift together the flour, baking powder, salt, cinnamon, and nutmeg. Combine the sugar and oil, then beat in eggs, one at a time. Stir in vanilla. Add to flour mixture all at once and mix well.

Squeeze off walnut-size balls and roll in additional sugar. Flour your hands and flatten each cookie as thin as you can. Place on an ungreased baking sheet about 2 inches apart. Sprinkle tops with more sugar if necessary.

Bake for 12 minutes or until light golden. Cool on racks.

Makes 5 dozen

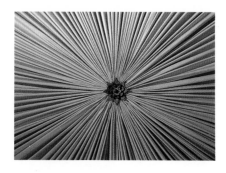

TOP: **Stitched bouquets.**
ABOVE: **Canopy bed interior.** RIGHT:
Victorian doll in its own chair.

Crawfish Dinner at Banker's House

BANKER'S HOUSE WAS SO NAMED because it was built in conjunction with the Natchez First Bank of Commerce in 1833. At the time, a law stipulated that the bank's officer, in this case a prominent local financier by the name of Levin R. Marshall, must live in the building with the deposits. As a matter of fact, the old steel vaults of the N. F. B. C. still exist under two small bedrooms upstairs.

However, all this precaution and sleeping above the store—or stash—couldn't save the bank from insolvency, and it failed in the late 1800s. The house was vacated and became a Presbyterian Girl's School for a few years.

Later, Banker's House found fleeting fame as a boardinghouse, whose reputation was enhanced by a legend: in 1878, the James boys, Frank and Jesse, stopped at the establishment for a few days; this sojourn quite possibly marked the only time in their "careers" that the brothers were willingly offered the comforts and hospitality of a banker's house!

Shaded by magnolias, Banker's House faces the broad Mississippi River. In front are slate sidewalks made from ballast used to stabilize the ships that regularly stopped at the landing below to take on produce and cotton.

Inside the two-story house, entered through a deeply recessed doorway flanked by classic sidelights (slim windows flanking a door) and Doric pilasters, there are beautifully carved overscaled pine moldings in pineapple bud and acanthus leaf patterns, both symbolizing hospitality. This motif is carried out on both the doors and windows. The black marble mantels and cypress flooring are also original and still in tact.

In 1971, Banker's House was bought by Mr. and Mrs. Luther A. Stowers. Typical of many such houses, most of its furnishings are original to another, earlier house—in this case, Oakland. For generations, Oakland belonged to the Minor family, of which Mrs. Stowers is a descendant.

Among the heirlooms at Banker's House today are Mallard and Belter furniture, early Southern paintings, and a large mahogany bookcase in the library. But probably the star of the collection is in the dining room—a dark German sideboard, heavily carved with animal reliefs, which had to be brought to Natchez by flatboat.

Banker's House, a National Historic Landmark, has been open to the public on selected occasions since 1973.

D. G.

M E N U

Skillet Asparagus

Smothered Crawfish
with Ham Stuffing

Boiled Rice

French Bread with Sweet Butter

Deep-Dish Dewberry Pie
with Cream

Wine · Coffee

THE MEAL BANKER'S HOUSE STANDS on a comparatively small plot of land and is literally surrounded by the downtown office buildings of Natchez. It is unique among the houses you will see here, for unlike the others, it is more a city or townhouse. And unlike places such as Stanton hall, it was obviously built for modest family comfort rather than as an ostentatious display of wealth, or to secure someone's social position.

But of course, when I say *modest,* the term is used in comparison to other houses of the period. By today's standards it would be considered quite large.

When we were mulling over what sort of meal to serve at Banker's House, we decided it should be something a family might have for a special occasion. Nothing fancy, but hearty, unpretentious fare. And since it was spring and the crawfish were jumpin', we figured a dish using these delicious local morsels was just the ticket.

The most popular way of eating crawfish, when not simply boiled like river shrimp, is to make a thick soup or stew of them with plenty of juice to dip your French bread in. And that's exactly what we did, adding our own version of ham stuffing to round it off. Such dishes are really very rich, and when served over rice, which we also did, are practically a meal in themselves. The only accompaniment is a salad or vegetable first course. With that in mind, we opted for fresh asparagus, quickly steamed, to start the meal.

Following the smothered crawfish was a luscious deep-dish dewberry pie with cream for dessert. And after *that* a cup of good strong Southern coffee to finish was more than welcome.

All in all, it's the kind of satisfying meal that invites you to take a quick turn around the block afterwards—or a nice little nap.

SKILLET ASPARAGUS

This is one of my very favorite ways of cooking asparagus—easy and delicious.

2 **pounds fresh asparagus, trimmed with ends peeled**

2 **tablespoons unsalted butter**
 Salt
 Lemon wedges
 Sliced hard-boiled eggs for garnish

Wash the asparagus. Melt the butter in a large skillet, then place the asparagus in with the water still clinging to it. Cover tightly and cook over medium heat, shaking pan occasionally, for 5 minutes. Check to be sure they are not scorching and cover again. Continue to cook for another 3 minuts. Obviously the timing will vary according to how thick the asparagus is and how well done you like it. I pre-fer mine crisp-tender. Season to taste with salt and serve with lemon wedges. Garnish with egg slices and chopped yolk.

Serves 6

PRECEDING SPREAD, LEFT: **Overscaled interior molding.** PRECEDING SPREAD, RIGHT: **Banker's House.** ABOVE: **1725 Continental desk and Victorian brass inkstand in the front living room.** LEFT: **Skillet Asparagus.**

SMOTHERED CRAWFISH with HAM STUFFING

For those of you who live where crawfish are difficult to find, you can substitute shrimp.

24 crawfish, steamed (see Note)

HAM STUFFING

4 tablespoons (½ stick) unsalted butter

¼ cup finely chopped onions

¼ cup finely chopped green bell peppers

¼ teaspoon dried thyme

¼ teaspoon dried marjoram

¼ teaspoon cayenne pepper

¼ cup finely chopped ham

½ cup soft bread crumbs

¼ cup beer, approximately

SMOTHERED CRAWFISH

½ cup (1 stick) unsalted butter

4 cups coarsely chopped onions

2 large cloves garlic, minced

2 cups coarsely chopped green bell peppers

3 cups coarsely chopped celery, with some tops

2 pounds peeled crawfish tails, with fat from heads (see Note)

½ cup coarsely sliced green onions, with some green tops

½ cup chopped fresh parsley

½ teaspoon cayenne pepper

½ teaspoon freshly ground black pepper

¾ teaspoon salt

1 teaspoon Tabasco

1 teaspoon Worcestershire sauce

1 teaspoon paprika

½ cup beer

Separate the crawfish heads from the tails. Peel the tails and set aside for the main dish. Clean out the heads, leaving the claws attached.

To make the stuffing, melt the butter in a small skillet and add the onions, green peppers, thyme, marjoram, and cayenne pepper. Sauté over medium-low heat about 5 minutes, or until wilted but not browned. Place ham and bread crumbs in a bowl and add sautéed vegetables. Toss to mix, adding beer to moisten. Stuff each crawfish head with 1 to 2 tablespoons of the stuffing, and set them aside.

To make the main dish, melt the butter in a large Dutch oven and add the onions, garlic, green peppers, and celery. Sauté over medium-low heat for about 20 minutes until soft. Mix in the crawfish tails, plus the tails set aside from the stuffing, the crawfish, fat, and then the green onions, parsley, cayenne, black pepper, salt, Tabasco, Worcestershire sauce, paprika, and beer. Fold together well. Place the stuffed heads on top of this mixture and cook, covered, for 10 more minutes. Turn heat down to very low and continue cooking for an additional 20 minutes, moving mixture around to make sure it doesn't scorch.

Remove the stuffed heads before serving and stir mixture well.

Serve over boiled rice in a soup bowl, garnished with the stuffed heads.

Serves 6

NOTE: If you can't get whole crawfish, substitute very large escargot shells to stuff, or very small lobster heads if you remember to save them the next time you steam lobster. And if you would like a little more sauce in the main dish, or the sauce is too thick, thin with a little chicken stock.

DEEP-DISH DEWBERRY PIE with CREAM

Dewberries are small wild berries in the blackberry family. You may also substitute strawberries for the dewberries. However, blackberries are the best substitute.

CRUST

2	**cups all-purpose flour**
½	**teaspoon salt**
1	**teaspoon sugar**
¾	**cup (1½ sticks) unsalted butter, chilled and cut into bits**
5	**tablespoons ice water**

FILLING

5	**cups dewberries (or blackberries), fresh or frozen**
2	**tablespoons all-purpose flour**
1	**cup plus 1 tablespoon sugar**
4	**tablespoons (½ stick) unsalted butter, chilled and cut into small pieces**
1	**tablespoon freshly squeezed lemon juice**
½	**teaspoon ground cinnamon**
	Heavy cream

Preheat the oven to 425 degrees. To make the crust, place the dry ingredients in a food processor and give it a few whirls to mix. Add the butter and process until mixture resembles coarse meal. With machine running, add water a tablespoon at a time, until dough holds together. Gather dough into a ball and place between 2 sheets of waxed paper, flattening the ball slightly. Refrigerate for 30 minutes.

To make the filling, wash and drain the berries. Place in a large bowl. Mix flour and 1 cup of the sugar, and sprinkle over berries. Add butter and lemon juice. Combine carefully with a wooden spoon.

Roll out half the dough on a floured surface and line an 8-inch deep-dish pie pan. Fill with the berry mixture. Roll out remaining dough and lay over filling. Seal sides and make steam slits in the top. Mix the remaining tablespoon sugar with the cinnamon and sprinkle on top. Bake for 35 to 40 minutes, until crust is dark golden.

Serve with cream.

Serves 6 to 8

OPPOSITE: **Smothered Crawfish with Ham Stuffing.** ABOVE: **Deep-Dish Dewberry Pie with Cream.** LEFT: **English silver teapot made by Crespin Fuller in 1806.**

Summer Dinner at Mistletoe

MISTLETOE, NESTLED IN THE Natchez countryside, has belonged to the same family for more than 180 years. Scotsman John Bisland settled near Natchez in 1776, hoping to find wealth in American agriculture. His instincts were right, and prosperity followed for the family.

Mistletoe was built in 1807 as a honeymoon cottage for Bisland's scholarly son, Peter, and his wife, Barbara. The younger Bislands seem to have shied away from the family business, mostly to concentrate on travel, academic pursuits, and the landscaping of their property. The couple occupied their small country manor until Peter was tragically involved in a fatal accident.

Mistletoe is admired for its simplicity and livable scale. Typical of planter-style architecture of the period, it has one and a half stories, a sharp sloping roof, square columns, and a wide, bannistered front gallery. Its entrance, also typical, is crowned by a half-moon fan light flanked by rectangular side panels, each with their original British rolled glass. Its trademark wrought-iron hardware, brass knobs, and escutcheons are still used inside.

The unique cypress rooms have corner fireplaces with high mantels, and all windows throughout the house are oversized. Today, the house is furnished with early New England furniture, mostly in the Queen Anne style, and the walls are hung with family portraits. There are extensive collections of Natchez coin silver and Old Paris china.

A large dining room was added in 1847 on the east side, as was a long gallery, since glassed in. Then, in 1849, the Bislands also added Mistletoe's present kitchen and bedroom wings to the rear of the house, closely following the original design and using materials saved from early outer buildings. These new wings created a two-level courtyard, which contains the original cistern.

The protected courtyard is now planted with jasmine, yellow roses, orange trees, orchids, and other semitropical plants, which would have probably pleased the first horticulturally minded Bisland.

Mistletoe has been shown to the public on selected occasions since 1942 and is now owned by Mr. and Mrs. James W. Overton and the family of W. P. Lambdin, Bisland descendants. It is listed in the National Register of Historic Places.

D. G.

TOP: **Family rooster.**
ABOVE: **View of the front garden.** OPPOSITE: **In the drawing room, looking out to the garden.**
OVERLEAF: **The front garden.**

MENU

Iced Beet and Orange Soup

Butter-Rum Shrimp

Yellow Rice

Green Beans in Mustard Marinade

Melba Toast

Peach Sherbet

Honey-Butter Snaps

Wine · Coffee

THE MEAL THE FIRST THING YOU are aware of when you visit Mistletoe, aside from its pleasing symmetry, is the profusion of flowers in its gardens. Then you notice that the gardens are enclosed by an unobtrusive fence. This is because the owners love their flowers, but they also love to have farm animals around for their grandchildren.

In the high brick-walled garden at the back of the house, the air is full of hummingbirds, attracted by half a dozen feeders. A peaceable kingdom.

Inside, on one side of the house, is a long, narrow dining room, with light cascading through its generous, tall windows. This room was too enticing to pass up, so that's where we decided to have a light summer dinner meal.

Not only is the combination of beets and orange a pleasing one, but the soup is a great color. I think this one is best served chilled.

The main course was shrimp. Shrimp are so versatile and plentiful in this part of the country that they are cooked in myriad ways, so here is one more. Accompaniments were simmered rice and marinated string beans.

Melba toast was served along with both the soup and the main course. We placed thinly sliced white bread in a very low oven (about 225 degrees) for about an hour, until the slices were golden.

In keeping with the lightness of the meal, we decided to make peach sherbet instead of the peach ice cream, so often the choice when peaches are in season. As an accompaniment to the sherbet, we served honey-butter cookies.

ICED BEET AND ORANGE SOUP

This soup freezes well if you have any left over.

- 3 **pounds beets, peeled and cut into thin slices**
- 1 **cup chopped onions**
- 1 **teaspoon dried basil**
- 4 **cups chicken stock**
- 2 **cups freshly squeezed orange juice**

Place all ingredients except orange juice in a saucepan and simmer over medium heat until beets are tender, about 15 to 20 minutes. Cool and purée. Add orange juice and chill.

Serves 8

OPPOSITE: **Hummingbird.**
ABOVE: **Iced Beet and Orange Soup.** LEFT: **Grandchildren's horse.**

BUTTER-RUM SHRIMP

5 tablespoons butter or margarine

48 large shrimp, peeled and deveined

Pinch of salt

¼ teaspoon coarsely ground black pepper

4 tablespoons chopped green onions, some tops

1 teaspoon dried tarragon

3 tablespoons light rum

In a skillet large enough to hold the shrimp, melt 2 tablespoons of the butter over medium heat. Add the shrimp, salt, and pepper, and sauté for 2 minutes, tossing gently until shrimp turn bright pink. Remove with a slotted spoon and set aside.

Melt the remaining 3 tablespoons butter in the skillet, add the green onions and tarragon, and sauté over medium heat for 3 minutes. Add the rum, stirring constantly to deglaze, and cook for 30 seconds. Return the shrimp and any liquid they have released to the pan and cook for another 30 seconds, or until the shrimp are thoroughly heated.

Serve over Yellow Rice (recipe follows).

Serves 8

OPPOSITE ABOVE: **Family silhouettes.** OPPOSITE BELOW: **Butter-Rum Shrimp, Yellow Rice, and Green Beans in Mustard Marinade.** RIGHT: **In the dining room.** BELOW RIGHT: **Summer butterfly.**

GREEN BEANS IN MUSTARD MARINADE

- 1 tablespoon dried rosemary
- 2 pounds fresh green beans, washed and snapped
- 1 teaspoon coarse-grained mustard
- 1½ teaspoons red wine vinegar
- 4½ tablespoons extra-virgin olive oil
  Salt and freshly ground black pepper

Fill a 1½-quart saucepan with water and bring to a boil. Add the rosemary and boil rapidly for about 2 minutes. Toss in the beans and continue to boil for about 10 minutes, or until the beans are crisp without being tough. As soon as the beans are done, drain them and rinse with cold water to stop the cooking process. Drain and set the beans aside.

To make the marinade, combine the mustard, vinegar, and oil in a small bowl. Whisk together, and add salt and pepper to taste. Dry the beans and toss them in the marinade. Refrigerate until ready to serve.

Serves 8

YELLOW RICE

- 2 tablespoons butter or margarine
- 1 teaspoon loosely packed saffron
- 2 cups long-grain rice (not instant)
- 3 cups water
- ½ teaspoon salt

Melt the butter in a saucepan over medium heat, add the saffron, and stir. Add the rice, stir well, then add the water and salt. Bring to a boil. Cover and cook over low heat for about 18 minutes, or until rice is tender and all the liquid has been absorbed.

Serves 8

NOTE: You can add more saffron and salt to taste, if desired.

BELOW: **Natchez silver coffeepot made by George MacPherson in 1845.** BOTTOM: **Detail of the garden gate.** RIGHT: **Peach Sherbet and Honey-Butter Snaps.** OPPOSITE: **Grazing sheep.**

PEACH SHERBET

8 large ripe peaches

2 teaspoons freshly squeezed lemon juice

2 cups water

1 cup sugar

¼ cup dry sherry

1 cup whipped cream

Slip the skins off the peaches by dipping them briefly into boiling water. Thinly slice to have about 2 cups.

Purée the peaches with the lemon juice. Boil the water, sugar, and sherry over low heat for 5 minutes, then stir in the purée. Cool and fold in whipped cream.

Freeze in an ice-cream freezer according to manufacturer's instructions.

Makes 1 quart

HONEY-BUTTER SNAPS

2¼ cups all-purpose flour

1½ teaspoons baking soda

½ teaspoon salt

¼ teaspoon ground cloves

¾ cup (1½ sticks) unsalted butter

1 cup firmly packed light brown sugar

1 egg

¼ cup honey

Preheat the oven to 350 degrees. Sift together the flour, baking soda, salt, and cloves and set aside. In a large bowl with an electric mixer, cream the butter until fluffy. Beat in the sugar gradually, then add the egg and beat in. Add the honey. On low speed, gradually mix in the sifted dry ingredients until just blended. Cut a piece of foil to cover 2 baking sheets, and drop the batter in well-rounded teaspoonfuls 3 to 4 inches apart. Bake for about 14 minutes, or until brown.

These cookies will be soft at first, but will crisp as they cool. Cool on racks. Store in an airtight container.

Makes approximately 36

Lunch in the Belvedere at Monmouth

MONMOUTH, ORIGINALLY BUILT
in 1818 by John Hankinson of
Monmouth County, New Jersey, was not
occupied long by Hankinson and his wife,
who succumbed to yellow fever. In the
following years, Monmouth lay neglected
until John Anthony Quitman, a newly
arrived lawyer from New York, purchased
the house and property in 1826. Still
an impressive and stalwart two-story
common-bond brick house with massive

square pillars, Monmouth was generally
considered to be one of the most eligible
sites in Natchez. With his purchase, Quitman gained immediate acceptance into
Natchez society, and took a local beauty,
Eliza Turner, for his wife.

Among Monmouth's architectural
details were heavy three-paneled doors
and intricate pilasters. These were
restored, along with the other deteriorat-
ing parts of the interior, and became the

setting for a fine collection of rare books and other furnishings.

In restoring the house, the Quitmans followed the Greek revival fashion by adding details of the style and a gracefully curved stairway. And outside, several two-story dependencies were erected along with smaller outbuildings to be used by Monmouth's large household staff.

John Quitman was one of the most respected lawyers in Mississippi, but he is best remembered for his heroism as a major general in the Mexican-American War. Returning a national hero, he was elected chancellor of Mississippi before being elected governor in 1849.

He continued to be idolized by his supporters until his untimely death nine years later. An outspoken Cuban sympathizer, Quitman was rumored to have been poisoned at a banquet for President James Buchanan in Washington, D.C.

Knowing he was dying, Quitman asked to be brought home to Monmouth. His funeral was one of the most mournful Mississippi had ever seen. Flags were flown at half-staff, businesses were closed, and soldiers wore black sleeve bands.

Today, Monmouth is owned by Mr. and Mrs. Ronald Riches of Los Angeles, who, like the Quitmans, had the task of completely restoring the house, after purchasing it in 1980. They have been scrupulous in replicating Monmouth's original details both inside and out, giving particular attention to the gardens.

Monmouth has been on the Pilgrimage tour intermittently since 1932 and is listed in the National Register of Historic Places.

D. G.

Tarragon Creamed River Shrimp and Chicken

Cat Head Biscuits

Rosemary String Beans

Melon and Grape Salad with Honey-Mustard Dressing

Plum Jam Cake with Rum Whipped Cream

Iced Tea or Wine · Coffee

THE MEAL BACK FROM THE MAIN road in Natchez proper, Monmouth stands at the center of a great expanse of well-tended rolling lawn. The town grew up around the house, but because it included so much land, its pristine setting was preserved. And unlike other local houses that were similarly surrounded over the years, this one, situated on a small rise so far away, allows you the pleasure of seeing it from a distance—just as a visitor might have done in the nineteenth century.

Toward the back are manicured gardens and a belvedere (summerhouse) overlooking a quiet pond, with blooming trees planted around its banks. It's hard to believe that just beyond the trees is a thriving community.

This summerhouse, with its tranquil view, was so tempting, the weather so warm and fine, that we served lunch outside rather than in the dining room.

Creamed chicken has always been a popular luncheon dish here, so we decided to start with that and add river shrimp to the recipe, along with the sweet tang of red peppers and tarragon. Creamed chicken is often served with rice, but a friend had told us about something called Cat Head Biscuits, so we substituted those. The vegetable was string beans simmered in a bit of rosemary water.

Chicken and shrimp together in a sauce is so rich and satisfying that you really don't need much more than a green salad to complete the meal. However, it is traditional to serve sweet salads with lunches in Natchez, so here we added a delicious combination of fruits with a honey-mustard dressing.

Finally, the dessert was a cake spread with plum jam. The traditional filling is mayhaw jam, made with the tart local fruit, but we substituted a jam that's easier to find.

Top the cake with rum-spiked whipped cream if you like, or keep the cake plain to have later with more iced tea. A perfect lunch for a balmy spring day.

PRECEDING PAGES: **Monmouth Plantation.** ABOVE: **Back entrance into the hall.** OPPOSITE ABOVE: **Tarragon Creamed River Shrimp and Chicken, and Cat Head Biscuits.** OPPOSITE BELOW: **Close-up of the main course.**

TARRAGON CREAMED RIVER SHRIMP AND CHICKEN

You might substitute crawfish tails for the shrimp, if you have them.

- ¾ cup (1½ sticks) unsalted butter
- ½ cup chopped green onions, including some green tops
- 1 teaspoon dried tarragon
- 1 cup chopped sweet red peppers
- 2 cups thickly sliced fresh mushrooms
- ¾ cup dry white wine
- 2 cups coarsely chopped chicken breast meat
- 2 cups small peeled and deveined river shrimp (or any very small shrimp)
- 2 tablespoons flour
- 2 cups half-and-half, scalded
  Salt and freshly ground white pepper
  Dash of nutmeg (optional)
  Dash of paprika (optional)

In a large saucepan, melt ¼ cup of the butter. Add the green onions and half the tarragon. Sauté over medium-low heat about 5 minutes, until onions are wilted. Add the red pepper, mushrooms, ½ cup of the wine, and the chicken. Increase heat to medium-high and sauté about 5 minutes, until chicken is opaque. Add the shrimp and remaining tarragon. Sauté, tossing constantly, for 2 minutes, until shrimp turn pink. Remove from heat and set aside.

In a separate saucepan, melt the remaining ½ cup butter. Sprinkle flour over it when the butter bubbles and whisk to mix well. Add half-and-half, whisking vigorously over medium-low heat until sauce is smooth and thick. Flavor with remaining ¼ cup wine and salt, pepper, and nutmeg. Continue to cook, whisking, for 2 minutes. Do not let boil.

Meanwhile, bring the chicken-shrimp mixture back to a simmer and add the sauce. Adjust seasonings. Serve hot on a split, buttered biscuit. Sprinkle with paprika.

Serves 6 to 8

TOP: **Belvedere set for lunch.** ABOVE: **Flowers at the foot of a garden statue.**

CAT HEAD BISCUITS

These are actually called "Carrie Bass's Cat Head Biscuits" whenever they are mentioned.

> 2 cups all-purpose flour
> 1½ teaspoons baking powder
> 1½ teaspoons sugar
> ⅓ cup solid vegetable shortening, cut into walnut-size pieces
> 1 cup buttermilk
> Unsalted butter, melted

Preheat the oven to 450 degrees. Lightly grease 2 baking sheets.

Combine the dry ingredients and shortening in a food processor. Process until the mixture has the texture of coarse cornmeal. Add the buttermilk and process, using a pulse motion, until mixture is moistened. (This can also be done by hand, using 2 knives to cut in shortening.) Turn dough out onto a floured surface and knead lightly 3 or 4 times.

"Choke off" 10 small pieces of dough; roll and flatten each into a ½-inch-thick round ("about the size of the average house cat's head," to quote the lady herself). Brush each top with melted butter and bake for 12 minutes or until golden.

Makes 10 large biscuits

ROSEMARY STRING BEANS

If you don't like the flavor of rosemary, these are not for you. In that case, just cook the string beans your favorite way.

- **2 quarts salted water**
- **3 tablespoons dried rosemary tied in a piece of cheesecloth**
- **2 pounds string beans, snapped with tips and stems removed**
- **Unsalted butter (optional)**
- **Salt to taste (optional)**

Bring salted water to a boil and add the rosemary. Simmer for 15 minutes, then add the beans and boil slowly for 15 to 20 minutes, depending on how tender you like them. Top each serving with a dab of butter and a sprinkle of salt, if you wish.

Serves 6

LEFT: **Lace curtains in the drawing room.**
ABOVE: **Music corner.**
ABOVE RIGHT: **Rosemary String Beans.**

MELON AND GRAPE SALAD with HONEY-MUSTARD DRESSING

Of course, almost any combination of melon will work, but in this case, watermelon and cantaloupe are awfully good.

- 1 **cup cubed cantaloupe**
- 1 **cup cubed and seeded watermelon**
- 2 **cups green seedless grapes**
- 5 **tablespoons lime juice**
- ½ **cup honey**
- 2 **tablespoons Dijon-style mustard**

Toss fruit with 1 tablespoon of lime juice and refrigerate, covered. When ready to serve, pour out any liquid, drying out the serving bowl. Whisk together the remaining lime juice, honey, and mustard. Toss with the fruit.

Serves 6

TOP: **Melon and Grape Salad with Honey-Mustard Dressing.** ABOVE: **Drawing room detail—the portrait is of a relative of General Lafayette.** RIGHT: **Blue damask chair in the drawing room.**

PLUM JAM CAKE with RUM WHIPPED CREAM

You can use any flavor of jam you like, but because the cake is rather sweet, a tart jam is best.

This recipe comes from Sister Mesick, one of the local ladies.

- 1 cup (2 sticks) unsalted butter, softened
- 2 cups granulated sugar
- 3¼ cups all-purpose flour
- 2 teaspoons baking powder
- ⅔ cup milk
- 8 egg whites
- 1 teaspoon almond extract
  Plum jam (or any flavor you like)
- ¼ cup confectioners' sugar

Preheat the oven to 350 degrees. Grease and lightly flour three 8-inch round cake pans.

Cream the butter until light and add 1 cup of the sugar. Cream again until very light in color.

Sift together the flour and baking powder. Add to the creamed mixture, alternating with the milk and mixing thoroughly. The batter will be very stiff.

Beat the egg whites until they start making soft peaks. Add the remaining sugar ¼ cup at a time, beating after each addition. Fold half the egg whites into the batter, then fold in the remaining whites and the almond extract. Pour into the prepared pans and bake for 25 to 30 minutes, or until cake tester comes out clean.

To assemble, melt the jam over low heat and spread on the bottom layer, allowing it to run over the sides. Repeat with the next 2 layers (holding them in place with toothpicks). Sprinkle with confectioners' sugar.

Serves 10 to 12

RIGHT: **Waterford crystal gas chandelier in the downstairs hall.** BELOW: **Plum Jam Cake with Rum Whipped Cream.**

Buffet Party at Oakland

OAKLAND, BUILT FOR CAPT. AND Mrs. Horatio Sprague Eustis, in 1835, once stood on the gigantic Alexander Moore estate, which reportedly encompassed more than 150 miles of land from Mississippi to Louisiana.

Eustis, Rhode Island native and Harvard graduate, came to Natchez to tutor the daughter of wealthy Natchezian Henry Chotard. Young Catherine eventually became Eustis's wife.

The house, which takes its name from the many live oaks that originally shaded the property, was built in an era when Greek revival architecture dominated the South. But Eustis sought simplicity and kept the more opulent aspects of this style to a minimum. Later, the Victorian influence of pretense and ornamentation also bypassed Oakland, which today remains very much as it was when first erected. This was a house meant to be lived in simply.

The front façade, a wide colonnaded gallery with floor-to-ceiling windows, is flanked by two wings. The stucco exterior was made to resemble stone.

The main entrance doorway is topped by a rectangular overhead light, and both the door and gallery windows are protected with heavy, hand-cut storm blinds.

Inside, ceilings are over sixteen feet high, and mahogany sliding doors with silver hardware separate the large rooms. Uncarved white marble mantels were used throughout the house in keeping with its theme of simplicity. The library is distinguished by its vaulted ceiling and paneling.

The house was built over a very large basement, unusual for its two cistern rooms. Nearby, a narrow winding stairwell leads down to a cool, white room once used to store milk. In the back of the main house stands a two-story brick dependency.

The house was sold in 1857 to Mrs. Eustis's cousin, John Minor. Both were relatives of the last District governor under Spanish rule, Stephen Minor.

John Minor was once described by Julia Nutt of Longwood as, "a very superior gentleman—who spent his life fox-hunting and giving dinner parties." Nevertheless, during the Civil War, Minor offered his home for Union sympathy meetings, which must have taken considerable courage and conviction.

Descendants of John Minor lived at Oakland for generations until it was sold by Mr. and Mrs. Al Graning in 1961 to Mr. and Mrs. Lawrence A. Adams, its present owners, who carefully restored Oakland to its former genteel simplicity.

Though Oakland is furnished with some original pieces, it also includes furniture from Homewood, an antebellum house that burned in the early 1940s.

Oakland, listed in the National Register of Historic Places, has been shown to tourists for over fifty years.

D. G.

MENU

Baked Stuffed Ham

Warm Curried Fruit

Purée of Beets and Carrots

Steamed Caraway Cucumbers

Kiss Rolls with Sweet Butter

Berry Sherbet

Wine · Coffee

THE MEAL THE FIRST THING YOU notice about Oakland is its openness—its gloriously proportioned triple-hung windows, unadorned, which flood its front rooms with warm reflected light.

Furnished in a fresh, spare way with graceful antiques, Oakland seemed the ideal setting for an early evening buffet supper. So that's precisely what we had.

Southerners especially, it seems to me, have a weakness for ham. And since a single baked ham can feed lots of guests with comparatively little preparation (if you don't go the clove-studding route, which I never do), it seemed the natural thing to build a buffet party around. This particular version was filled with savory mushroom stuffing; and because something sweet is traditional with ham hereabouts, we came up with warm curried fruit.

The vegetable accompaniment could have been almost anything, but our choice was a purée of beets and carrots (a beautiful color), which incidentally is a good make-ahead combination. Unlike many plain steamed vegetables, purées do not risk being overcooked when reheated.

For crunch there were steamed cucumbers tossed in butter with caraway seeds.

Also traditional with ham in Natchez are simple "ice box" rolls. These particular ones are called Kiss Rolls because they come out resembling two lips.

Finally, since this menu included a fair number of dishes, we assumed most guests would not really be in the mood for a big dessert, but would instead welcome something light and refreshing to finish the meal (and to cleanse the palate)—hence the berry sherbet. Actually, any sherbet would be appropriate here.

PRECEDING SPREAD, LEFT: A spectacular drawing-room window. PRECEDING SPREAD, RIGHT: Oakland ABOVE: Sideboard set with the buffet supper. FAR LEFT: Rare Stewartia blossom. LEFT: The back courtyard.

BAKED STUFFED HAM

Be sure to have your butcher do the deboning. It will save you plenty of time, especially if you have never done it before. (Save the bone and end for cooking any kind of beans. It may be frozen for later use.)

10- **to 12-pound cooked ham, deboned with joint end removed**

Savory Stuffing (recipe follows)

½ **cup coarse-grained mustard**

¼ **cup dry white wine**

½ **cup firmly packed dark brown sugar**

Preheat the oven to 350 degrees. Cut the rind from the ham and remove excess fat. Score remaining fat. Stuff lightly, being careful not to pack stuffing in. Truss and place in oven, and cook about 20 minutes, until fat begins to brown.

Meanwhile, combine mustard, wine, and brown sugar to make a paste. Smear this over the browned ham and continue to bake for another 25 minutes, basting several times with pan juice.

Serves 12 or more

SAVORY STUFFING

4 **tablespoons (½ stick) unsalted butter**

1 **cup coarsely chopped onions**

½ **cup chopped green bell peppers**

4 **cups coarsely chopped mushrooms**

½ **teaspoon dried sage**

½ **teaspoon dried thyme**

½ **cup chopped fresh parsley**

Generous ¼ cup coarsely chopped walnuts

2 **cups coarse fresh bread crumbs, toasted**

½ **teaspoon freshly ground black pepper**

½ **teaspoon salt**

3 **to 4 tablespoons dry white wine**

Melt butter in a large skillet and sauté onions and green peppers about 5 minutes, until onions are wilted. Add mushrooms and sauté over low heat for another 15 minutes. Stir in all other ingredients except wine, remove from heat, and toss. Mix in wine, tossing again.

If any stuffing is left over, place in a shallow greased baking dish and bake, covered, along with the ham. Uncover for last 15 minutes of cooking time to lightly brown stuffing.

Makes about 4 cups

STEAMED CARAWAY CUCUMBERS

Cucumbers are too often thought of as something just to have in a salad. Here is a change of pace.

6 **large cucumbers, peeled, cut in half lengthwise, and seeded**

2 **teaspoons caraway seeds**

1 **tablespoon unsalted butter**

1 **tablespoon plain yogurt**

Salt

Cut cucumbers into ½-inch-thick half circles. Sprinkle with caraway seeds, then place in a large steamer. Steam about 20 minutes, until tender. Remove to a warm bowl and toss with the butter and yogurt, adding more of either, if you like. Salt to taste.

Serve warm or hot.

Serves 12

PURÉE OF BEETS AND CARROTS

The thing to remember about this, and most other purées, is that it is important to season them to your personal taste. They can be puréed to a completely smooth texture or be left rather coarse, as you wish.

You can use crème fraîche, butter, yogurt, or a little stock to achieve the consistency and taste you like. A squeeze of lemon or a few drops of vinegar will also pique the flavor of most vegetables.

- 3 cups grated carrots
- 3 cups coarsely chopped, peeled baked beets (see Note)
- 1½ tablespoons freshly squeezed lemon juice
- ⅛ teaspoon grated nutmeg
- 4 tablespoons (½ stick) unsalted butter
- 2 tablespoons plain yogurt or sour cream
  Salt

Place the carrots in a small pot and just barely cover with water. Bring to a boil and cook slowly for about 15 minutes, until tender. Drain and place in a food processor along with all other ingredients except salt. Purée to desired consistency. Add salt to taste and more of any of the other ingredients you desire.

Reheat in the top of a double boiler, stirring as it heats.

Serves 12

NOTE: To bake beets, trim stems, leaving about ½ inch of tops. Leave root on. Preheat the oven to 400 degrees and line a pan with foil. Place the beets in pan and close with foil. Bake an hour or so, until tender when pierced with the point of a knife. Timing depends on the size and age of the beets. Allow to cool enough to handle, then cut off stems and roots. The skins will slip off.

KISS ROLLS

Obviously, you could make these rolls into any shape you like, but I like them as they are.

- ¾ cup milk
- ¼ cup sugar
- 1¼ teaspoons salt
- 4½ tablespoons unsalted butter, plus additional softened butter
- 2 envelopes active dry yeast
- ¾ cup warm water (about 110 degrees)
- 4½ cups all-purpose flour

Scald the milk, being careful not to let it scorch, and stir in the sugar, salt, and butter until butter melts. Set aside to cool slightly. Place yeast in a large mixing bowl and pour in the warm water, then stir to dissolve. Add the milk mixture, then stir in half the flour, beating and stirring until smooth. Mix in the remaining flour. (This may be done in a mixer with a dough hook.)

Knead the dough, either in a mixer or turned out onto a floured surface, for about 8 minutes, or until smooth and elastic. Put dough in a buttered bowl, cover with a tea towel, and allow to stand in a warm, draft-free spot for about 1 hour, or until doubled in bulk.

Punch dough down and roll out to about ¼ inch thick. Cut into 1-inch rounds, spread rounds lightly with additional softened butter, and fold in half with butter inside. Place on ungreased baking sheets and let rise for 45 minutes.

Meanwhile, preheat the oven to 425 degrees and bake rolls for 15 to 18 minutes, or until just turning golden.

Makes about 40

OPPOSITE: **Baked Stuffed Ham and Steamed Caraway Cucumbers.** TOP: **Kiss Rolls.** LEFT: **Through the window into the drawing room.** ABOVE: **White summer rose.**

WARM CURRIED FRUIT

You might also want to add a cup or so of freshly grated coconut to this sometime.

- 2 cups thickly sliced, peeled, and cored pears
- 2 cups thickly sliced, peeled, and cored apples
- 2 cups thickly sliced, peeled and pitted peaches
- 2 cups coarsely chopped fresh pineapple
- 2 cups seedless grapes
- 2 generous tablespoons fresh curry powder
- ⅓ cup (⅔ stick) unsalted butter, slightly softened
- ¾ cup firmly packed light brown sugar

Preheat the oven to 325 degrees. Mix fruit in a large bowl and set aside. Mix curry powder, butter, and brown sugar then toss with the fruit. Scoop out fruit into a shallow, buttered baking dish.

Bake, covered, for 45 minutes. Uncover and continue baking for another 15 minutes, until fruit is soft.

Serve warm.

Serves 12

BERRY SHERBET

The good thing about this sherbet is that you can use any kind of frozen or fresh berries—raspberries, blackberries, blueberries, or a mixture.

- 4 cups berries
- ¾ cup sugar
- 1 cup water
- 1 tablespoon vodka
- 2 egg whites, lightly beaten
  Fresh berries, for garnish (if available)

Place the berries in a small saucepan and heat, stirring occasionally, for 10 minutes, or until the juice is rendered out. Push berries through a sieve to remove seeds (if using raspberries or blackberries; this is not necessary with blueberries). Discard seeds and set juice aside.

Place sugar and water in a saucepan and bring to a simmer. Simmer slowly for 10 minutes. Combine juice and vodka with syrup, then allow to cool. Stir in the egg whites and freeze in an ice-cream freezer according to manufacturer's instructions.

Serve garnished with extra berries if they are fresh.

Serves 12

TOP: **Original Oakland mirror from the 1830s.**
CENTER: **Elizabethan-era painting on wood.**
ABOVE: **Etched ladies' dresser set.** OPPOSITE:
Berry Sherbet.

Lunch Under the
Trees at Edgewood

EDGEWOOD, CONSTRUCTED DUR-
ing the early 1850s, is unique,
resembling no other mid-nineteenth-century Natchez house. It lacks the design
solemnity of its Greek revival neighbors
and the informality of the raised cottage.

Instead, builder Thomas Rose chose to
make Edgewood Italianate, with square,
bold lines and gingerbread-ornate detailing
—quite unlike another of his commissions,
Stanton Hall, which he conceptualized.

In front are two stories with eight
Corinthian columns forming a long gallery. The back, however, is made up of
three levels, the lowest of which originally
housed the kitchen.

Inside, Edgewood has fifteen-foot ceilings and a grand entranceway with a
graceful stairway, an unexpected visual
treat considering the comparative modesty
of the exterior. Interestingly, the house's
basic architecture has remained virtually

unchanged since its completion, except for modern conveniences added over the years.

But speaking of conveniences, Edgewood has the distinction of being the only antebellum house in Natchez that had indoor plumbing when it was built. Another innovation was an elaborate dumbwaiter. Family meals arrived in the dining room from the kitchen on the lower level while still piping hot.

The pink stuccoed house still stands in its original terraced setting. The gardens and giant trees have matured over the last century, making the site even more beautiful.

Edgewood was planned for Samuel Lambdin and his wife, Jane Bisland, whose family lived in nearby Mount Repose. Its name derives from its location at the southwest portion of the Bisland family estate, which included Mistletoe and Mount Repose. This vast tract was located in the Pine Ridge section.

Long after the Civil War, many descendants of the freed slaves who had worked the plantation lived in Edgewood's outbuildings. And the Lambdins themselves lived in the house for more than 100 years. However, in 1951, it was purchased by Mr. and Mrs. Richard A. Campbell, who have filled it with rare eighteenth-century English antiques and continued its legacy of gracious living.

Edgewood is listed in the National Register of Historic Places.

D. G.

M E N U

Carrot and Sweet Red Pepper Soup

Natchez Seafood Salad

Bread Sticks with Tabasco Butter

Melon with Blueberry Sauce

Iced Tea or Wine · Coffee

BLOOMING SHRUBS AND neatly trimmed stands of trees suddenly give way to green open vistas on the long, winding drive up to Edgewood. This is even before you glimpse the house, all pink stucco and white trim, standing on a small rise. If you turn when you reach the front entrance, you'll see a great swath of lawn rolling in the direction from which you have just come.

Each time you visit there, gardeners are busy. This is a place whose owners obviously love their special and serene landscape.

So, as beautiful as the interior of Edge-

wood was, we just couldn't resist setting up a table for our lunch in the center of a growth of towering cedar trees. The day was warm, but there was a constant current of air moving the limbs to cool us.

As you see, we started off with a smooth carrot and sweet red pepper soup. I like it served slightly chilled, but it is also very good at room temperature—and on this day, it got that way fast.

Soup was followed by the star of the meal, a seafood salad made from typical Natchez ingredients: spicy boiled shrimp, crabmeat, and crawfish tails. Everyone down here is partial to seafood, and their salads are delicious; but what I think made this particular version so tasty was that the shrimp were boiled in that fiery mix of herbs and spices so favored in the Gulf states. After cooking, the shrimp were added to the onions and marinated overnight.

The crabmeat one buys in Natchez is backfin lump, which is precooked but unseasoned—just as well, because the shrimp is so potent it can stand a milder ingredient for balance. And of course the ubiquitous crawfish tails have a very strong and distinctive flavor no matter how they are prepared.

Along with the salad were fresh bread sticks with Tabasco butter. I have a real weakness for this butter and like it on almost anything.

Finally, dessert was melon with blueberry sauce. Melons are particularly sweet here, where the summers are so hot. It's said that the hotter the weather, the sweeter the melon—one of nature's thoughtful compensations.

PRECEDING SPREAD, LEFT: **Edgewood.** PRECEDING SPREAD, ABOVE: **Under the cedar trees.** PRECEDING SPREAD, BELOW: **Bearded iris.** FAR LEFT: **Carrot and Sweet Red Pepper Soup under the trees.** LEFT: **The serene drawing room.**

CARROT AND SWEET RED PEPPER SOUP

For a slightly heartier soup on another occasion, you might try adding cooked shrimp and serving it warm.

- 6 cups grated carrots
- 3 cups milk
- 2 sprigs fresh savory
- 6 cups homemade or canned chicken stock
- 4 large sweet red peppers
- ½ cup coarsely chopped red onions
- 2 teaspoons freshly squeezed lemon juice
- ¼ teaspoon each salt and freshly ground black pepper, or to taste

    Sour cream, plain yogurt, or crème fraîche, for garnish

Combine the carrots, milk, 1 savory sprig, and half the chicken stock in a saucepan. Simmer for 15 minutes over medium heat.

Meanwhile, roast peppers under broiler, turning occasionally, until skins blacken. Set aside in a closed paper bag.

Strain the carrots from milk and set aside, reserving liquid. Peel and seed peppers. Chop coarsely and heat in remaining stock along with onions and remaining savory sprig. Simmer rapidly over high heat for about 10 minutes. Lower heat to medium and add reserved carrots and cooking liquid, lemon juice, and salt and pepper. Heat for 5 minutes. Do not boil. Allow to cool, then purée in batches. Serve hot or cold, garnished or plain.

Serves 8 to 10

NATCHEZ SEAFOOD SALAD

You could add or substitute scallops or lobster in this recipe if you live in an area where they are plentiful. Should you do this, though, remember to cook and marinate one of the ingredients as the shrimp are here.

SHRIMP

- 6 quarts water
- ½ cup salt
- 4 fluid ounces Zatarain's Crab Boil
- 1 tablespoon black peppercorns
- 6 lemons, halved
- 2 medium onions, quartered
- ¾ pound fresh medium shrimp

MARINADE

- ¼ cup rice wine vinegar
- ¼ cup German Riesling wine
- 2 teaspoons chopped fresh basil
- ½ teaspoon minced garlic
- 1 teaspoon Dijon-style mustard
- ½ teaspoon salt
- ½ teaspoon freshly ground black pepper
- 1 cup olive oil
- ½ cup chopped sweet red or Vidalia onions

CRAWFISH

- 1 pound peeled crawfish tails
- 3 lemons
    Salt to taste

SALAD ASSEMBLY

- 1 pint fresh backfin lump crabmeat, carefully picked over
    Capers, grated hard-boiled egg, minced green onion tops, or minced chives, for garnish
    Homemade mayonnaise

To cook the shrimp, boil the water, spices, lemons, and onions for 30 minutes. This is a strong concoction so I advise not only turning on the vent but vacating the kitchen until the 30 minutes are up. People here often do this in the yard. Add the shrimp and cover the pot. Remove from heat immediately. Allow to steep for 5 minutes, then pour shrimp into a colander and cover with ice to stop the cooking. Peel and devein when cool.

OPPOSITE: **The entrance hall.** BELOW: **Natchez Seafood Salad and Bread Sticks.** BOTTOM: **Queen Anne settee (probably Dutch), circa 1725.**

To make the marinade, purée vinegar, wine, basil, garlic, mustard, salt, pepper, and olive oil in a food processor or blender. Place shrimp in a bowl and toss with chopped onions. Pour marinade over all and cover. Refrigerate overnight.

To steam the crawfish tails, fill the bottom of a small steamer with water. Cut lemons in half and add to water. Place crawfish tails in the top of the steamer and cover. Bring to a boil and steam for 10 minutes. Cool.

To assemble the salad, drain marinade from shrimp and toss shrimp with crawfish and crabmeat. You can also add a few capers and, if you like, grated hard-boiled egg and minced green onion tops or chives on top. Serve with mayonnaise on the side.

Serves approximately 8

BELOW: **Lilies.** BOTTOM:
**Silk-covered Sheraton
drawing-room sofa.**
OPPOSITE TOP: **Melon with
Blueberry Sauce.**
OPPOSITE BOTTOM: **Louisiana
iris.**

BREAD STICKS with TABASCO BUTTER

- 3 cups all-purpose flour
- 1 package active dry yeast
- 1 tablespoon sugar
- ¾ teaspoon plus 1 teaspoon salt
- 1 cup warm water (about 110 degrees)
- 1 tablespoon light oil, such as safflower or sunflower oil
- Tabasco Butter (recipe follows)

In a food processor fitted with a steel blade, combine 1½ cups of the flour with the yeast, sugar, and ¾ teaspoon salt. With machine running, add water and oil. Add the balance of the flour and process until mixture forms a ball.

Divide dough into 4 portions and each of these into 10 balls. Form each into a "rope" by rolling between hands. Coat baking sheets with cooking spray and arrange ropes evenly, leaving about ½ inch between. Cover with a lightly dampened cloth. Allow to rise in a warm place for 50 minutes. These will not double in bulk, but will expand.

Preheat the oven to 400 degrees.

Sprinkle ropes with remaining teaspoon of salt and bake for 25 minutes. Serve with Tabasco Butter.

Makes about 40 sticks

TABASCO BUTTER

- 1 cup (2 sticks) unsalted butter, softened
- ½ teaspoon Tabasco

Whip the butter with a wire whisk or hand mixer until fluffy, adding Tabasco as you go along. Scrape into a small crock. Refrigerate until ready to use.

Makes 1 cup

MELON with
BLUEBERRY SAUCE

We call for honeydew melon here because it is plentiful in Natchez, however you can substitute any melon that's ripe.

- 2 **cups fresh blueberries**
- ½ **cup sugar**
- 2 **tablespoons freshly squeezed lemon juice**
- 1 **tablespoon vodka**
  Dash of ground cinnamon (optional)
- 1 **very large honeydew melon, peeled, seeded, and cut into medium-thin slices**

Place the berries, sugar, lemon juice, vodka, and cinnamon in a small saucepan. Bring to a simmer over medium heat, and cook slowly for 20 minutes. Cool, cover, and refrigerate until ready to use.

Arrange melon slices on individual plates and put a line of sauce down the middle of each.

Serves 8

Sunday Dinner at Cherokee

CHEROKEE STANDS HIGH ABOVE the streets of Natchez's Garden District. It shares the same hillside where American soldiers in 1798 transferred the Natchez area from its European governor to the newly formed Mississippi Territory.

A short while before, Cherokee's construction had begun on the site, which was a portion of the 1794 Spanish land grant made to Ebenezer Rees. Cherokee was built on a hillside because early property laws prohibited the leveling of hills for building houses. People at the time believed that yellow fever germs thrived just beneath the soil, and that to disturb them would wreak havoc on the city. Consequently, nearly all French and Spanish houses of the era were perched on the territory's abundant hillsides and cliffs.

Cherokee, named for the Indians who lived throughout Mississippi at the time, was originally a simple eighteenth-century brick house. In 1810 it was purchased by David Michie, who expanded and remodeled it to suit his more modern tastes.

A front wing with fourteen-foot ceilings and a classic cove entranceway supported by Doric columns was added, as well as moldings beautifully carved in the Greek honeysuckle motif. A short hallway was also constructed to connect the newer rooms to the older ones, which became bedrooms and a music room. Finally, a mahogany staircase was installed to connect the upper floor to the kitchen below.

Cherokee's hilltop location placed it where it could catch the welcome river breezes. Jib windows and large doors also made cross ventilation possible. And of course, the thick brick walls helped hold the cool evening air.

It was also about now that the formal garden was laid out in back of the house, a garden which still thrives and provides a shaded oasis for dining.

In 1845, Cherokee was purchased by Frederick Stanton, whose family lived in it until construction was completed on their nearby palatial new home, later named Stanton Hall.

After the Civil War, the house changed hands often, even once belonging to a Northern carpetbagger. By the end of the Depression, Cherokee had suffered the fate of so many of its contemporaries and was in almost complete disrepair. Fortunately, in 1939, Mr. and Mrs. Charles J. Byrne came to its rescue by purchasing the property and beginning the task of rebuilding. In the end their efforts had restored Cherokee to its former self. Today the house is owned by Mr. and Mrs. Hugh Junkin, Jr., whose Natchez ancestry dates back to the last century.

Cherokee, listed in the National Register of Historic Places, has been shown on Pilgrimage tours since 1940.

D. G.

MENU

Summer Garden Salad

Frogs' Legs with Parsley Butter

Okra Pilaf

Cumin Corn Bread

Fresh Figs with Cream

Ginger Snaps

Wine · Coffee

THE MEAL ALTHOUGH CHEROKEE IS one of the town's earliest houses, it is still surrounded today by the same beautifully kept gardens. And because they were so tranquil and shady, I was tempted to set up the dining table outside. But inside the house there's a small oddity, a room off the main dining room that was originally used as a ladies' morning room. Situated in such a way as to be flooded with bright early sunlight from two directions and looking across to the densely shaded neighboring houses, it was so charming that that's where we dined.

The first course was a refreshing summer garden salad, which was followed by frogs' legs in parsley butter.

Frogs' legs have always been popular in this part of the South and are still plentiful, although I imagine the current supply would seem meager by eighteenth-century standards. Even so, in other places they seldom seem to be served. Frankly, I think a lot of people tend to forget about them.

To go along with the frogs' legs we combined rice and okra, long-standing Southern staples, in one recipe. Then we added spicy corn bread to round out the menu.

Dessert was fresh figs, which were in season, bathed in cream. And someone suggested old-fashioned ginger snaps to go along with them—the kind that were so popular way back when. I hadn't thought of ginger snaps in ages, but I was glad to be reintroduced to them, as I bet you will be, too.

SUMMER GARDEN
SALAD

You can substitute any other combination of greens that you like.

DRESSING

- 1 teaspoon Dijon-style mustard
- ½ teaspoon honey
- 1 tablespoon freshly squeezed lemon juice
- 1½ tablespoons olive oil

SALAD

- 1 ounce slivered almonds
- ½ cup peeled, seeded, and coarsely chopped cucumbers
- ½ cup coarsely chopped yellow summer squash
- ½ cup coarsely chopped zucchini
- ½ cup chopped radishes
- ½ cup chopped green bell peppers
- 1 cup torn red leaf lettuce
- 1 cup torn romaine

To make the dressing, place mustard, honey, lemon juice, and olive oil in the bottom of a large salad bowl and whisk together. Toss lightly with all salad ingredients.

Serves 6 to 8

PRECEDING SPREAD, LEFT: **Shady back garden.** PRECEDING SPREAD, RIGHT: **Cherokee.** TOP: **The "small" dining room.** ABOVE: **Summer Garden Salad.**

FROGS' LEGS with PARSLEY BUTTER

In Natchez, frogs' legs are often served broiled. You could do them that way for this recipe after they have been marinated (and patted dry), if you prefer.

- 12 pairs frogs' legs
- 4 cups milk
- 4 cloves garlic, crushed
- 2 teaspoons Tabasco
  Oil for deep-frying
- 4 eggs
- 2½ cups all-purpose flour
- 1 tablespoon salt
- 1 tablespoon freshly ground black pepper
  Parsley Butter (recipe follows)

Divide the legs by cutting along the joint at the top of the thigh. Place legs in a large bowl with the milk, garlic, and Tabasco. Cover and marinate, refrigerated, overnight.

Heat oil to 400 degrees, preferably in a thermostatically controlled fryer. Place eggs in a bowl and beat lightly. Set aside. Mix flour, salt, and pepper in a plastic bag. Dip legs in egg, then allow excess to drain off. Shake in flour. Fry for 5 to 8 minutes (depending on their size). Legs will float, and bubbling will die down when done. They should be light brown with dark flecks. Serve topped with a dab of Parsley Butter.

Serves 6 to 8

PARSLEY BUTTER

- 1 cup (2 sticks) unsalted butter, softened
- ½ cup finely chopped fresh parsley, no stems

Place butter in a small bowl and sprinkle parsley over all. Whip with fork until combined. Scrape into a crock. Use softened.

Makes approximately 1¼ cups

TOP: **View through the front door.** ABOVE: **Frogs' Legs with Parsley Butter and Okra Pilaf.** OPPOSITE TOP: **Garden steps.** RIGHT: **Fresh Figs with Cream, and Ginger Snaps.**

OKRA PILAF

I know a lot of people think they don't like okra. If you are one of them, try this and you might change your mind.

- 1 teaspoon salt, or to taste
- 1 cup plus 3 tablespoons long-grain rice (not instant)
- 2⅓ cups chicken stock
- 1 tablespoon unsalted butter, approximately
- 2 cups medium okra rings

Add the salt and rice to the chicken stock and bring to a boil. Turn back to very slow boil and cook, uncovered, for 10 minutes. Test for doneness. If not tender, give it another minute or so. Drain and toss with the butter.

While rice is cooking, steam okra about 5 minutes, until tender. Toss with the rice, adding more salt and butter if you like.

Serves 6

CUMIN CORN BREAD

This corn bread is also good with fish.

- 1 cup stone-ground yellow cornmeal
- 1 teaspoon salt
- ¾ cup all-purpose flour
- 1½ teaspoons baking powder
- 2½ teaspoons sugar
- ½ teaspoon ground cumin
- 1 egg
- 1 cup milk
- 1 tablespoon unsalted butter, melted

Preheat the oven to 425 degrees. Generously grease a 10-inch cast-iron skillet. Mix the dry ingredients, then combine egg, milk, and butter. Stir milk mixture into dry ingredients and mix until completely moist. Pour into skillet and bake for 25 minutes, until golden.

Serves 6 to 8

FRESH FIGS with CREAM

What a treat these are!

- 20 small, fresh figs, stemmed and peeled
- 1½ to 2 cups heavy cream
- Grated lemon rind (optional)

Cut each fig in half and divide the lot evenly among 6 or 8 individual serving dishes. Pour 4 tablespoons of cream over each. Sprinkle with a little finely grated lemon rind if you like.

Serves 6 to 8

GINGER SNAPS

I had forgotten how good these can be when they are thin and freshly baked.

- ¾ cup solid vegetable shortening, butter, or margarine, or a combination
- 1 cup sugar
- ¼ cup maple syrup
- 1 egg, lightly beaten
- 2 cups all-purpose flour
- 2 teaspoons baking soda
- 1 teaspoon ground cinnamon
- 1 teaspoon ground ginger
- Sugar for coating cookies

Preheat the oven to 375 degrees. Grease 2 baking sheets. Cream the shortening and sugar together until fluffy. Beat in the syrup and egg. Sift dry ingredients together, then add to creamed mixture and mix well. Roll into walnut-size balls. Roll each in additional sugar. Place 2 inches apart on baking sheets and bake for 15 minutes, until dry and lightly browned.

Makes approximately 4 dozen

Vegetable Dinner at Green Leaves

GREEN LEAVES IS APTLY NAMED, since its city block–long plot is dotted by giant oak trees, one of which is thought to be 400 years old. Legend has it that this giant's sheltering canopy was a gathering place for the Natchez Indians.

The Greek revival house began as a small, elegantly proportioned, white raised cottage, built in 1838 by E. P. Fourniquet. A decade later it was sold to the Koontz-Beltzhoover family, whose six generations of descendants have lived there ever since.

George Washington Koontz, who purchased Green Leaves from Fourniquet,

was responsible for the extensive early remodeling that transformed it into the sprawling house it is today. He added two side wings, creating an enclosed garden in the back, and extended the bannistered gallery on all three sides. Adjacent rooms all opened onto this heavily planted courtyard. He also added wrought iron–trimmed balconies.

Koontz formed a banking partnership with William Britton, which still flourishes today. During the Civil War, Koontz became a trusted friend of Confederacy President Jefferson Davis, who sent him abroad to negotiate loans for the struggling South. However popular he may

have been before the war, bitter feelings went hand-in-hand with Reconstruction, and a banker's job, especially Koontz's, was not universally admired. The Confederacy had used its own currency during the war emergency and after defeat, Confederate money was worthless. People who had traded U.S. bills for it were not reimbursed. Even today, a bullet hole in the transom of Green Leaves' front doorway is witness to an attempt to assassinate Koontz after the war.

LEFT: **The great oak in the backyard.** ABOVE: **Green Leaves street entrance.**

Green Leaves' comfortable interior did, however, survive the economically devastating war without having to be sacrificed for cash. Richly detailed Greek revival moldings are still intact throughout the house, as are the gilt cornices, Italian black marble mantels, and bronze chandeliers. Much of the original Empire and rococo revival furniture remains, and even the wallpaper in the front parlor is unchanged.

However, there are two possessions that are particularly treasured by the family. One is a French sword passed on to Col. Daniel Beltzhoover during the battle of Vicksburg by a fatally wounded Englishman, who said it had been used in the 1815 Battle of Waterloo. The other is an extensive set of china that, though unsigned, is said to have been decorated by John James Audubon.

Today, Ruth Audley Beltzhoover and her daughter and son-in-law, Mr. and Mrs. George Morrison, Jr., occupy the house.

Green Leaves is listed in the National Register of Historic Places and was one of the first houses to be opened to tourists in the early 1930s.

D. G.

MENU

Butter Beans with Bacon

New Potatoes and String Beans

Cream Peas

Black Crowder Peas

Stewed Tomatoes

Sliced Tomatoes

Turnip Greens

Yellow Squash and Onions

Fried Corn

Buttered Beets

Hot-Water Corn Bread

Peaches-and-Cream Cake

Iced Tea

 THE MEAL ENTERING GREEN LEAVES by the steep front steps rising directly from the street below —much as you do at Cherokee—a visitor can't help but notice its proximity to other houses. However, once you pass through the vast central hall and step down into the enormous walled garden at the back, you are transported to the country.

From this vantage, Green Leaves looks like a completely different house in a completely different setting. Here are stately old oak trees in a semiformal landscape partly embraced by the galleried wings extending on both sides from the main part of the house. One oak in particular is so large, especially in this sheltered space, that it is truly breathtaking. Flowers bloom in the borders along with fancy leaf caladiums, and hanging baskets overflow with ferns.

This strong bucolic feeling, combined with the fact that the house itself is a living family museum filled with photographs, portraits, furniture, and every manner of memento, suggested a classic menu. So we chose that long-standing Southern favorite, the vegetable dinner.

Now before you react to this long list of dishes, let me explain that only years ago would you have had such an extensive selection of vegetables at one meal. But we figured that as long as we were at it, we might as well go all the way.

Vegetable dinners, which are still popular in the South, are nowadays more often made up of maybe five or six at the most, along with corn bread. What the family particularly likes and what is available in season usually define the choice. For instance, in summer our vegetable dinners always included cornmeal-coated fried green tomatoes because they were a favorite of my father's.

Anyway, this is to give you an idea of some of the vegetables that might be included in such a meal and how they would be prepared.

I should add that these cooking methods run completely counter to the current fashion of serving vegetables almost raw. For years there has been a standing joke in the South about rushing to finish breakfast so that you could put the vegetables on in time for them to be done at noon.

ABOVE: **Black Crowder Peas.** OPPOSITE: **Black marble mantel in the drawing room.** OVERLEAF: **The dinner set out on the table, accompanied by Hot-Water Corn Bread and Peaches-and-Cream Cake.**

BUTTER BEANS
with BACON

These are smaller and have a different texture from their cousin, lima beans.

- **2 pounds fresh butter beans, shelled**
- **4 slices bacon**
- **5 cups water**
- **1 teaspoon sugar**
- **1 teaspoon salt**
- **1 teaspoon freshly ground black pepper**
- **3 tablespoons unsalted butter**

Wash the beans and set aside. Cut bacon into several pieces and sauté over low heat in a deep saucepan for 10 minutes. Drain off all but 2 tablespoons of the fat. Add water, beans, and all the other ingredients except the butter. Cook, uncovered, over medium heat for 30 minutes or longer, until very tender. Stir in the butter just before serving.

Serves 6

FRIED CORN

Use large-kernel corn for this recipe.

- **3 tablespoons unsalted butter**
- **2 cups corn kernels scraped from cobs (about 8 ears)**
- **1 teaspoon sugar**
  Salt and freshly ground black pepper

Melt the butter in a nonstick pan over medium-high heat. Add the corn and sprinkle with sugar. Stir, scraping from the bottom as starch browns, cooking for about 10 to 15 minutes over medium heat. Salt and pepper to taste. Serve hot.

Serves 6

HOT-WATER CORN BREAD

Another variation on the Southern staple.

- **2 cups yellow cornmeal**
- **1 teaspoon salt**
- **1 cup boiling water**
  Oil for frying

Mix the cornmeal and salt. Pour boiling water over and stir. Batter will be sticky and stiff. Roll batter into tablespoon-size balls and flatten with your finger.

Meanwhile, in a cast-iron skillet on the stove, heat about a ¼ inch of oil. Fry corn bread balls for about a minute on each side, or until they start to turn golden. Serve immediately.

Makes about 36

CREAM PEAS

These are like crowder, or field peas and are a relative of black-eyed peas, with a similar taste and texture.

- **2 pounds of cream peas, shelled**
- **2 cups cubed ham (2-inch cubes)**
- **5 cups water**
- **1 teaspoon sugar**
  Salt and freshly ground black pepper

Wash the peas and set aside. Starting in a cold pan, fry ham over low heat in a large heavy pot for 10 minutes. Add water, peas, and sugar. Simmer for 2 hours, until peas are soft. Add salt and pepper to taste. Remove peas from liquid with a slotted spoon and serve hot.

Serves 6

NEW POTATOES AND STRING BEANS

This is a really old-fashioned favorite.

- 5 cups string beans, snapped with tips and ends removed
- 4 slices bacon
- 2 cups coarsely chopped onions
- 16 very small new potatoes, scrubbed
- 8 cups water

Wash the beans and set aside. In a heavy pot, fry the bacon over low heat for 8 minutes. Add the onions and beans, and fry on low, stirring and lifting for another 10 minutes, until beans are bright green. Add the water and potatoes, and simmer over low heat for 2 hours. Remove vegetables from liquid with a slotted spoon and serve hot.

Serves 6

STEWED TOMATOES

Tomatoes are popular any way they are prepared in the South.

- 2 tablespoons (¼ stick) unsalted butter
- 2 cups coarsely chopped onions
- 2 teaspoons red wine vinegar
- 5 cups peeled and seeded tomatoes
- 1 teaspoon dried basil

Melt the butter over low heat in a deep saucepan. Add the onions and sauté for 15 minutes. Add the vinegar and sauté for another 2 minutes. Add tomatoes and basil. Cook for 2 hours over very low heat. Serve warm.

Serves 6

TURNIP GREENS

Turnip greens have a strong flavor, which I love. You can also combine them with other greens.

- 6 bunches turnip greens
- 4 slices bacon
- 2 tablespoons sugar
- ½ teaspoon salt
- ½ teaspoon freshly ground black pepper
- ½ cup water

Strip the leaves from the stems, discarding stems. Place leaves in a sinkful of water and swish them around.

Meanwhile, in a very large, heavy pot, cook the bacon over low heat for about 7 minutes, until translucent. Carefully lift greens from the water, shaking off excess, and add to the pot. Turn several times with a wooden spoon. Add sugar, seasonings, and water. Simmer over very low heat for 3 hours. Remove from liquid with a slotted-spoon and serve hot.

Serves 6

BLACK CROWDER PEAS

These are another of the myriad choices you have in fresh summer peas in the South.

- 2 pounds peas, shelled
- 3 strips salt pork belly (about ⅛ inch thick each)
- 1 small clove garlic, chopped
- 5 cups water
- 1 tablespoon sugar
  Salt

Wash the peas and set aside. Fry the salt pork over low heat in a large heavy pot for a few minutes to render out fat. Add the garlic and continue cooking over low heat for about 8 minutes; take care not to let the garlic get too brown. Add the water and peas. Simmer for 1½ hours, until very tender. Add sugar and salt to taste. Remove from liquid with a slotted spoon and serve hot.

Serves 6

YELLOW SQUASH AND ONIONS

You can cook zucchini this way, too.

- 4 tablespoons (½ stick) unsalted butter
- 4 cups coarsely chopped onions
- 8 cups medium sliced, young yellow summer squash, about 2 pounds
- 1 teaspoon sugar
- 1 teaspoon salt
- ½ teaspoon freshly ground black pepper
- ¼ cup water

Melt the butter in a medium saucepan over low heat. Add the onions, cover, and cook for 15 minutes, stirring occasionally to prevent sticking, until translucent but not browned. Add the squash, sugar, salt, pepper, and water. Cook for 1 hour, stirring occasionally until squash and onions are very tender. Remove from liquid with a slotted spoon and serve hot.

Serves 6

BUTTERED BEETS

You could also cook these in a hot oven if you like (see page 73).

- 16 small to medium beets
- 1 teaspoon sugar
- 1 teaspoon salt
- 2 tablespoons unsalted butter

Wash and cut tops from beets. Place them in a saucepan and cover with water. Add sugar and salt. Cook over medium heat for about 45 minutes, or until tender when pierced with the point of a knife.

Drain, peel, and cut in half. Toss with butter, and serve hot.

Serves 6

PEACHES-AND-CREAM CAKE

Make this cake when the peaches are dead ripe.

- 4 cups sifted cake flour
- 1 teaspoon salt
- 4 teaspoons baking powder
- 1½ cups (3 sticks) unsalted butter
- 3 cups sugar
- 8 eggs
- 1 cup milk
- 2 teaspoons vanilla extract
- 8 large peaches, peeled and sliced medium thin
- ¼ cup freshly squeezed lemon juice
- 1 quart heavy cream, whipped

Preheat the oven to 325 degrees. Grease and lightly flour two 9-inch square cake pans. Set aside.

Sift together the cake flour, salt, and baking powder. Set aside.

Cream the butter and sugar together until light and fluffy. Add the eggs, one at a time, beating well after each addition. Add the flour mixture, alternating with the milk, in 4 batches. Mix in the vanilla and pour batter into pans.

Bake in the center of the oven with both pans on the same rack (do not let pans touch) for about 25 minutes, or until a cake tester comes out clean.

Allow pans to sit for a few minutes before inverting cakes onto a cooling rack.

To assemble the cake, toss the peaches with the lemon juice. Cover the bottom cake layer with a thick layer of whipped cream. Place half the peaches on top, shaking the lemon juice off as you do so. Cover with top cake layer, holding it in place with toothpicks. Frost the top layer and sides with whipped cream. Place remaining peaches on top.

Serves 12

OPPOSITE: **Old Paris urn from 1831.** LEFT: **Games in the library.**

Lunch on the Screened Porch at Hope Farm

HOPE VILLA, ORIGINALLY A farmhouse, was a typically unassuming structure with low ceilings and a simple stairway. Today, known as Hope Farm, it reflects two very different architectural styles. Luckily, these styles work together to create a harmonious whole.

According to records, the first section was built around 1775, and reflects the English-influenced American architecture of the period. But when Hope Farm (Villa) was sold to the Spanish governor, Don Carlos de Grand Pre, in late 1789, a more elegant and spacious one-story house was built in front and connected to the original—thus enclosing a garden bounded on the front by the new house and on one side by the old house. Directly across from the old house, the cistern and pump house enclosed the third side. This new structure reflected Spanish taste, and created a suitably grand entrance for its owner.

But most intriguing today is Hope Farm's original structure. On its first floor are the kitchen, which is still filled with the day-to-day cooking equipment of the period, and a tiny furnished schoolroom.

In the early 1800s, Hope Farm passed from Don Carlos to George Overaker, who was later to own nearby Hawthorne.

Hope Farm is perhaps more famous locally as the home of the late Katherine Grafton Miller and her husband J. Balfour; it was Mrs. Miller who was instrumental in creating the Natchez Pilgrimage, thereby bringing tourists to Natchez during the Great Depression and infusing the city's economy with much-needed cash. The money made it possible for the owners of many of the grand old houses to restore and maintain them. Undoubtedly, some of the houses would not otherwise have survived the financial stresses.

The Millers bought Hope Farm in the 1930s, a few years before starting the Pilgrimage Garden Club. Together, they restored the house and gardens.

The influential couple died childless, but they were admired by generations of Natchez citizens for their kindness and civic service. One admirer, Ethel Banta, purchased the Miller's house in 1986, and now lives there with her family.

Naturally, Hope Farm has been open to tourists from the very beginning—1936—and is listed in the National Register of Historic Places.

D. G.

M E N U

Chopped Salad with Pepper Mayonnaise

Deep-Dish Ham and Eggplant Pie

Butter Beans

Pickled Okra

Peach and Meringue "Shortcake"

Iced Tea or Wine

Coffee

THE MEAL

AS SOON AS I WENT through Hope Farm, I knew where I would like to have a meal—on the screened porch running the entire width of the back.

Unfortunately, screened porches, which were so popular only a couple of generations ago, have given way in most houses to claustrophobic air-conditioning. I don't mean to say that air-conditioning doesn't have its uses, or that I would like to go back to those unrelieved sweltering days and nights, but it is a pity so many people have abandoned the pleasure of dining under a ceiling fan in the shaded and screened seclusion of a back porch. Especially when the weather breaks enough to allow you to do so in comfort.

And Hope Farm is just the sort of house where you would expect to find a screened porch intact. Even today it is an appealingly rustic place. Having grown and changed in the last century to accommodate changing styles and family needs, Hope Farm nonetheless still shows its modest—almost austere—beginnings proudly. It was a farm after all, not a mansion, and therein lies its charm.

Here is our version of a farm lunch, which began with a chopped salad dressed with pepper mayonnaise.

Then came a deep-dish pie of ham and eggplant. This is a combination that has always been very popular. Sometimes the two are used to stuff cabbage, and sometimes it is simply baked together. And many times the mixture is made so hot with cayenne pepper that you need a quick swig of iced tea after the first bite. No matter what form it takes, this combination is always welcome at Southern tables.

Butter beans have a mild flavor and gave this meal a nice balance. Incidentally, I have seen frozen butter beans here, but they don't seem to have caught on outside of their natural habitat. Their closest relative seems to be baby limas.

And because it is also quite usual for pickles and relishes to be part of a meal in the South, we served pickled okra.

Finally, with local peaches available every place, we selected the best of them and made a shortcake—one calling for meringues instead of the more typical sweet biscuit.

PRECEDING PAGE, LEFT: **Cool brick sidewalk.** PRECEDING PAGE, CENTER: **Grassy steps in the garden.** PRECEDING PAGE, RIGHT: **Hope Farm.** ABOVE: **Hybrid tea rose.**

TOP: **Chopped Salad with Pepper Mayonnaise.** ABOVE: **Plantation bell.**

CHOPPED SALAD with PEPPER MAYONNAISE

I know foodies will probably be horrified by the iceberg lettuce called for here, but that's what is used all over the South. Of course, you could substitute any crisp lettuce you fancy.

MAYONNAISE

- 2 egg yolks
- ½ teaspoon salt
- 1 teaspoon red wine vinegar
- ½ teaspoon freshly squeezed lemon juice
- ¾ cup vegetable oil
- ¼ cup olive oil
- 1 tablespoon freshly ground black pepper

SALAD

- 1 head iceberg lettuce, washed and coarsely chopped
- 2 very large tomatoes, peeled, seeded, and coarsely chopped
  Salt

To make the mayonnaise, in a food processor fitted with a steel blade, process the egg yolks, salt, and half the vinegar for a few seconds to mix.

With the machine running, add the balance of the vinegar, the lemon juice, and the oils in a thin stream, continuing until all is incorporated. Mix in pepper.

Toss lettuce and tomatoes with a little mayonnaise and arrange on individual serving plates. Salt to taste and serve remaining mayonnaise on the side.

Serves 8

DEEP-DISH HAM AND EGGPLANT PIE

If you have them, you could add crawfish tails or shrimp to this recipe.

CRUST

- 3 cups all-purpose flour
- 1 teaspoon salt
- ½ cup (1 stick) unsalted butter, frozen and cut into pieces
- ½ cup solid vegetable shortening, frozen and cut into pieces
- 6 tablespoons ice water

FILLING

- 5 cups peeled and cubed eggplant (1-inch cubes)
- 2½ cups water
- ½ teaspoon dried oregano
- ¼ teaspoon salt
- 2 tablespoons unsalted butter
- 1 medium onion, coarsely chopped
- 1 cup coarsely chopped green bell peppers
- 1½ cups corn kernels
- 1 cup coarsely chopped ham
- 1 egg, lightly beaten
- ¼ cup dry bread crumbs
- ½ cup freshly grated Parmesan cheese
- Additional salt and freshly ground black pepper

To make the crust, combine flour and salt in a food processor with a steel blade. Add butter and shortening. Process until the texture is like coarse cornmeal. Add ice water and process just until dough begins to form a ball. Divide in half and press portions into a flattened circle between sheets of waxed paper. Wrap and refrigerate.

Preheat the oven to 400 degrees. Roll out half the dough on a floured surface and line a deep 9- to 10-inch pie plate. Set aside.

To make filling, place eggplant in a deep saucepan, add water, and stir in oregano and salt. Simmer for 10 minutes, until just tender. This makes about 2 cups of cooked eggplant.

Melt the butter in a large skillet over medium heat. Add the onion and green peppers. Sauté until wilted, about 10 minutes. Add the corn and ham and sauté for an additional 5 minutes. Add the eggplant, mix, and then add egg; mix well. Sprinkle with the cheese and bread crumbs, mixing with a fork. Salt and pepper to taste.

Fill the pastry-lined baking dish with the eggplant mixture. Roll out remaining dough and lay over filling, carefully sealing to the bottom crust. Paint top with a little extra milk, make steam slits, and bake for 35 to 40 minutes, until top starts to turn light golden.

Serves 8

NOTE: The filling will make 3½ cups and will amply fill a deep 9- or 10-inch dish. If you have leftovers, cook in a small casserole for lunch.

PICKLED OKRA

If you don't want to make these, substitute commercial pickled okra.

This recipe comes from Laura Godfrey.

- 2 **pounds fresh, small okra (large will not do)**
- 1 **quart 5 percent distilled white vinegar**
- 2 **tablespoons salt**
- 1 **tablespoon Tabasco**
- 1 **tablespoon Worcestershire sauce**
- 5 **cloves garlic, peeled**
- 1 **tablespoon dried dill**
- 1 **tablespoon mustard seeds**
- 5 **small whole hot or mild peppers**

Wash the okra and soak for 1 hour in cold water. Meanwhile, sterilize and keep hot 5 pint jars and lids. Put the vinegar, salt, Tabasco, Worcestershire sauce, garlic, dried dill, and mustard seeds in a pot. Bring to a boil and boil for 5 minutes. Pack the okra, 1 pod up and 1 down, in the hot jars and add 1 pepper and 1 clove of garlic to each jar. Carefully cover with the boiling liquid and seal. Store in a cool, dry place.

Makes 5 pints

BUTTER BEANS

These can be cooked ahead of time and reheated.

- 2 **pounds fresh butter beans, shelled**
- 1 **tablespoon vegetable oil or bacon fat**
- 1 **small onion, minced**
- 5 **cups water**
- 1 **teaspoon sugar**
- 1 **teaspoon salt**
- 1 **teaspoon freshly ground black pepper**
- 3 **tablespoons unsalted butter**

Wash the beans and set aside. Melt oil or bacon fat in a deep saucepan, add the onion, and sauté about 8 minutes, until lightly brown. Add the water, beans, and all the other ingredients except butter. Cook over medium heat for 30 minutes or longer, until very tender. Drain and stir in butter before serving.

Serves 8

OPPOSITE: **Lunch on the back screened gallery.** ABOVE: **Deep-Dish Ham and Eggplant Pie, Butter Beans, and Pickled Okra.** RIGHT: **Close-up of the pie.**

PEACH AND MERINGUE "SHORTCAKE"

Here is a nice change from the usual shortcake. Use it with any kind of berry or other fruit.

- **3 egg whites, at room temperature**
- **⅛ teaspoon salt**
- **1 cup sugar, plus extra for cream**
- **1 teaspoon vanilla extract**
- **6 large peaches, peeled and sliced**
- **1 tablespoon freshly squeezed lemon juice**
- **1 pint heavy cream**
- **Vanilla extract or rum, for flavoring the cream**

Preheat the oven to 350 degrees. Lightly grease and barely flour a sheet of waxed paper. Place on a baking sheet. Set aside.

Beat egg whites until foamy. Add salt and beat until soft peaks begin to form. Continue beating while adding sugar, several tablespoons at a time, until mixture is stiff and shiny. Beat in vanilla, then drop by large spoonfuls onto waxed paper. Place baking sheet in oven and turn oven off. Leave in oven until meringues are completely cooled (or overnight).

Peel off paper and place them in an airtight container.

To serve, toss peaches with lemon juice. Whip the cream with a little extra sugar and vanilla or rum. Assemble as you would shortcakes.

Serves 6 to 8

Hunt Breakfast
at Dunleith

DUNLEITH, THE QUINTESSEN-tial Southern mansion, is one of the most photographed houses in the United States. Since it overlooks the main artery into the city, it is encountered by almost everyone who visits Natchez.

Rising on a terraced forty-acre plot, the main house is patterned after a Greek temple, surrounded by twenty-six Tuscan columns, supporting double galleries.

Built in 1856, it succeeded an earlier eighteenth-century house, known as Routhland, which was destroyed by a lightning fire a year before. The original

was part of a 700-acre Spanish land grant given to Job Routh, who built and eventually bequeathed the first house to his daughter and her new husband, Charles Dahlgren.

Dahlgren, who ultimately became a Civil War general, was a duel-fighting direct descendant of Sweden's King Gustavus Adolphus. And it was he who commissioned Maryland architect John Crothers to design the even more majestic 1856 Routhland.

The new house was composed of twelve large rooms with sixteen-foot ceilings and floor-length windows affording views of terraces and gardens from every

angle. Dahlgren filled the house with the best imported furnishings his fortune could buy, and then went on to add a poultry house topped by an open pigeonnaire, a castlelike Gothic-style carriage house with the stable underneath, and a greenhouse heated by an underground firebox. An eighteen-room servants' wing stood nearby.

BELOW: **Dunleith.** ABOVE: **The pigeonnaire.**

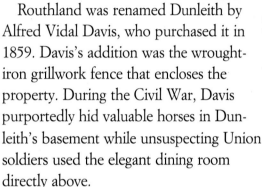

Routhland was renamed Dunleith by Alfred Vidal Davis, who purchased it in 1859. Davis's addition was the wrought-iron grillwork fence that encloses the property. During the Civil War, Davis purportedly hid valuable horses in Dunleith's basement while unsuspecting Union soldiers used the elegant dining room directly above.

By 1886, Dunleith had been sold to Joseph N. Carpenter, whose family remained there for five generations. The property's present owners, Mr. and Mrs. William Heins of Texas, refurnished it with eighteenth- and nineteenth-century English and French furniture, and they added to the dining room a Zuber wall mural printed from the original 1855 wood blocks, depicting the major temperate zones.

Now, with the house and surrounding buildings restored, the family has turned its attention to recultivating the elaborate gardens and grounds to ensure that Dunleith will charm future generations.

Dunleith is a National Historic Landmark.

D. G.

MENU

Smothered Quail

Baked Bouillon Grits

Buttered Steamed Slaw

Dunleith Biscuits

Blackberry-Walnut Conserve

Fig Preserves Ice Cream

Café au Lait

Wine

THE MEAL THE FIRST THING ONE admires about Dunleith is its stately symmetry, but the interior holds a lovely surprise: a glorious glow created by light pouring in on all sides through floor-to-ceiling windows. As you can imagine, these windows also afford breathtaking views of the gardens, through the branches of the great oaks planted over a century ago.

So what would be more fitting to enjoy in such a place than a hunt breakfast, that romantic and traditional (mostly) meal associated in many minds with the good life, nineteenth-century style? To tell you the truth, I don't think there are many

hunt breakfasts served these days, but this sumptuous menu would be perfect for any special breakfast party.

As you can see, the breakfast was centered around smothered quail, a dish that is tops on my list of favorite foods. When I was a child, we used to have quail often, so it has a nostalgic association.

And, of course, with the quail there had to be grits, here baked in bouillon, which gives it a rich, nutty flavor. Also a must

are biscuits. Luckily the present cook at Dunleith had her own special recipe for the dough, which she lightened by stretching it and gently tossing it in the air, the way chefs do pizza dough—although she didn't go in for any high-flying feats. Whatever, she swore her technique works, and the biscuits sure tasted good. Naturally, there had to be plenty of sweet butter and preserves to go with them.

To this combination we added steamed slaw, not classic in any way, but marvelously fresh tasting and a nice balance for all the rest. This was accompanied by wine for those who wanted it, but also by the more usual café au lait. Finally, the dessert was a smooth fig ice cream.

If this meal doesn't make you hum *Dixie,* I don't know what will.

SMOTHERED QUAIL

Salt and pepper

12 **quail (allow 2 per person)**

¼ **cup safflower oil**

10 **tablespoons (1¼ sticks) unsalted butter**

¾ **cup plus 5 tablespoons all-purpose flour**

1 **teaspoon paprika**

1 **teaspoon freshly ground black pepper**

½ **teaspoon dried marjoram**

½ **teaspoon grated nutmeg**

½ **teaspoon dried thyme**

½ **teaspoon dried sage**

½ **cup finely chopped onions**

½ **cup finely chopped celery**

½ **cup finely chopped carrots**

3 **cups hot chicken stock**

⅓ **cup dry red wine**

Season birds inside and out. Set aside. Heat oil and 2 tablespoons of the butter in a large skillet over medium heat. Mix the ¾ cup of flour with remaining dry ingredients and dredge quail. Shake off excess. Place quail in skillet and fry evenly. Cook for 20 minutes, until quail are golden brown with darker flecks.

In a large Dutch oven, melt the remaining 8 tablespoons butter over medium heat. Add vegetables. Sauté for 5 minutes, until vegetables are wilted, then sprinkle remaining 5 tablespoons flour over all and cook about 15 minutes, until flour turns reddish brown, turning and stirring all the while. Do not let flour burn. When flour is dark, whisk in hot stock gradually until smooth. Add wine and simmer over low heat for 5 minutes. Add quail and cover. Cook over very low heat for 1½ to 2 hours, until birds are tender but not yet falling apart. Add more liquid if necessary.

Serves 6

BUTTERED STEAMED SLAW

We cooked this in a microwave oven, which frankly, I haven't had much experience with. However, it worked wonderfully. Of course, you can get the same results with a covered skillet.

- 1 **medium head green cabbage, chopped as for slaw**
- 1 **tablespoon rice wine vinegar or freshly squeezed lemon juice**
- ½ **teaspoon salt**
- ½ **teaspoon freshly ground black pepper**
- ½ **teaspoon sugar (optional)**
- 2 **tablespoons unsalted butter**

Toss all ingredients together in a glass bowl and cover tightly with plastic wrap. Make a steam vent in the plastic wrap using a knife or fork. Place in a microwave oven. Cook on HIGH for 5 minutes. Let stand for 2 minutes. Slaw should be crisp-tender; if it isn't, give it another minute.

You may also heat this in a covered skillet over very low heat for about 10 minutes, or until slaw reaches the degree of doneness you like.

Serves 6 to 8

BAKED BOUILLON GRITS

This is sort of a grits soufflé.

- 4 **cups chicken stock**
- 1 **cup quick grits (not instant)**
- ½ **teaspoon salt**
- 4 **eggs, separated**

Preheat the oven to 350 degrees. Generously grease a 2-quart soufflé or Pyrex baking dish. Bring the stock to a boil in a large saucepan and stir grits in slowly. Add salt and after it has returned to a boil, simmer for 5 minutes. Remove from heat and cover. Let stand for 5 minutes.

Meanwhile, beat the yolks until light yellow; whisk the whites until they stand in peaks. Combine yolks with grits, then fold in whites. Pour into a baking dish and bake for 20 to 25 minutes, until puffy and light golden. Serve immediately.

Serves 6

DUNLEITH BISCUITS

These make excellent shortcake biscuits if you increase the sugar to ⅓ cup, then brush the tops with milk and sprinkle with sugar before baking.

- 1½ **cups all-purpose flour**
- 1 **teaspoon salt**
- 3 **teaspoons baking powder**
- 2 **tablespoons sugar (optional)**
- 1¼ **cups solid vegetable shortening**
- 1¼ **cups milk**

Preheat the oven to 350 degrees. Grease a baking sheet.

Mix the dry ingredients and then cut in the shortening with a pastry blender or 2 knives. Mix in the milk, then knead by hand, lifting and lightly tossing dough into the air, stretching it as you do. Roll on a lightly floured board to about 1 inch thick. Cut into 3-inch rounds and bake for 15 to 20 minutes or until golden.

Makes 18

BLACKBERRY WALNUT CONSERVE

The ubiquitous blackberry once more —and how perfectly their flavor combines with walnuts to make this tart and crunchy conserve.

- 12 **to 16 ounces fresh or frozen blackberries**
- ½ **cup sugar**
- 1 **tablespoon freshly squeezed lemon juice**
- 1 **jigger (2 tablespoons) vodka**
- 1½ **cups coarsely chopped walnuts**
- ¼ **teaspoon ground cinnamon (optional)**

Combine the berries, sugar, lemon juice, and vodka in the top of a double boiler. Stir and cook over low heat for 20 mintues or until thickened. Mix in walnuts and cinnamon. Allow to cool and store, tightly covered, in the refrigerator.

Makes about 2 cups

FIG PRESERVES ICE CREAM

You can use store-bought fig jam or make your own fig preserves, which are very easy.

- **2 cups milk**
- **2 eggs**
- **1 cup sugar**
- **1 tablespoon vanilla extract**
- **1 cup heavy cream**
- **1 cup Freddie's Fig Preserves (recipe follows)**

Scald the milk. Meanwhile, beat the eggs and sugar together until lemon-colored. Add a little of the milk to the mixture to heat it, then pour into hot milk, stirring all the while. Continue to cook over very low heat (or in a double boiler) about 10 minutes, or until thickened. Whip cream and fold in. Mix in preserves.

Pour into an ice-cream freezer and freeze according to manufacturer's directions.

Makes about 1 quart

FREDDIE'S FIG PRESERVES

This is my Aunt Freddie's recipe.

- **5 pounds small fresh figs, stemmed**
- **5 cups sugar**
- **1½ lemons, seeded and thinly sliced**

Wash the figs in cold water. Place in a heavy pot with the sugar and just enough water to cover the sugar and keep figs from sticking. Stir. Add the lemon slices and cook over moderate heat about 10 minutes or until syrup is thick and fruit is tender. Skim off foam that comes to the top. When the juice has become a syrup, divide among sterilized jars and seal. Turn jars upside down to ensure perfect seal. Process in boiling water for 5 minutes.

Makes 8 ½-pint jars

CAFÉ AU LAIT

There is nothing mysterious about making café au lait. Just be sure your coffee is strong and freshly brewed (never instant). Sweeten it to taste and add milk that has been allowed to come just to a boil. The traditional proportion is half milk and half coffee, but it's really a matter of personal taste.

TOP: **Classic magnolia blossom.** ABOVE: **Café au Lait.** OPPOSITE: **Fig Preserves Ice Cream.**

Formal Dinner at Montaigne

MONTAIGNE, SO BEAUTIFUL today, was once the temporary dwelling of white scalawags and newly freed homeless blacks during the Civil War. The original builder, lawyer William T. Martin, had left to serve in the Confederate army and his family fled in fear of the Union troops starting to occupy Natchez. Poachers set up camp inside Montaigne's elegant walls, and horses were made comfortable along with them.

The family managed to save much of the original furniture, but what remained was callously used by the soldiers for kindling. Chandeliers were smashed, leaving crystal scattered over the lawn. Silver and brass were melted down and lost forever. The gardens were trampled in an orgy of destruction.

Returning from the war, Martin found his house in ruins, along with his fortune, now faltering with the failing Southern economy. But undaunted, Martin revived his law practice, and with the help of his wife and their thirteen children, set about making Montaigne home again.

Today, with its Georgian architecture and serene landscape restored, Montaigne, named after Martin's French heritage, is the soul of unpretentious sophistication. Its central hallway, with black-and-white parquet tile floor and grisalle-colored landscape wallpaper, sets the tone for the house. Marble mantelpieces, oversized windows, and generous wood moldings remain unchanged, even though a minor portion of the house's interior was remodeled in neoclassical style in 1927, including the graceful winding stairway in the central hall.

Several families lived in Montaigne after Martin died and the family dispersed, until it was purchased in the spring of 1935 by the late Mrs. Joseph W. Kendall and her son and daughter-in-law, Mr. and Mrs. William J. Kendall, all of whom were instrumental in the early organization of the Natchez Pilgrimage.

Following Martin's lead, William Kendall amassed a collection of more than 350 varieties of camellias and japonicas in Montaigne's gardens.

The salmon-pink stucco house sits in a seclusion of towering trees not far from downtown Natchez; it is still occupied by Mrs. Hunter Goodrich, the former Mrs. William J. Kendall, whose ancestry in the Natchez area dates back to 1792.

Montaigne is listed in the National Register of Historic Places.

D. G.

OPPOSITE: **The dining room set for dinner.** BELOW: **Montaigne.**

M E N U

Yellow Squash Soufflé with Fresh Tomato and Sweet Red Pepper Sauce

Pan-Sautéed Catfish Fillets with Parsley-Pecan Sauce

Lemon Carrots

Green Salad (Optional)

Chess Pie with Blackberry Sauce

Wine · Coffee

THE MEAL MONTAIGNE'S CONFIdently stylish rooms, with their serene colors and antique furniture gathered over the years, are subtle examples of a living, lovingly used, period interior. The house expresses reverence for the past, but its ongoing vitality and purpose still manage to be uncompromisingly of the present.

I especially liked having glimpses of the "life" of the house all around: portraits of family members, past and present; photographs taken over the years; books everywhere; games and tapes tucked away on tea paper-lined shelves; music piled on the piano; ferns and flowers tumbling out of urns and small vases; personal mementos filling the glass-doored shelves of a beautiful secretary.

The house is a warm and inviting place.

Yellow squash baked in a light soufflé and served on a generous pool of fresh tomato and sweet red pepper sauce started the meal—a treat for the eyes as well as the palate. Next came catfish fillets, sautéed and then topped with a parsley and pecan pestolike sauce. The fish was accompanied by lemony carrots.

Should you like, you could certainly add plain boiled potatoes sprinkled with chopped chives and parsley, or buttered rice, to this meal, but frankly I don't think it is necessary.

A modest green salad might be served with a small wedge of cheese before going on to dessert, which was the classic chess pie—a favorite all over the South for generations. To enhance the pie we added a fresh blackberry topping. However, if you don't have blackberries, use any other type of berry, or a combination of berries.

YELLOW SQUASH SOUFFLÉ with FRESH TOMATO AND SWEET RED PEPPER SAUCE

Zucchini squash can be substituted for the yellow squash.

- 2 cups sliced yellow summer squash (1-inch rounds)
- 1 cup coarsely chopped onions
- 9 tablespoons unsalted butter
- 1 tablespoon sugar
  Salt and freshly ground black pepper
- 6 tablespoons all-purpose flour
- 2 cups milk, scalded
  Dash of nutmeg
- 1 tablespoon cornstarch
- 1 tablespoon water
- ¼ teaspoon cayenne pepper
- 2 teaspoons Worcestershire sauce
- 8 eggs, separated
  Fresh Tomato and Sweet Red Pepper Sauce (recipe follows)

In a saucepan, combine the squash, onions, 4 tablespoons of the butter, sugar, and salt and pepper to taste. Cover with water and bring quickly to a boil. Simmer about 45 minutes, until vegetables are very tender. Drain, mash, and set aside. You should have about 1½ cups of pulp.

Preheat oven to 400 degrees and butter a 2-quart soufflé dish. Set aside.

Melt remaining 5 tablespoons butter in a saucepan over moderate heat until small bubbles form. Whisk in flour well. Add milk in a steady stream, whisking rapidly, until sauce is thick and smooth. Add salt and pepper to taste and a dash of nutmeg. Cook for one or two minutes more. Combine cornstarch and water to make a paste, add to sauce and stir. Cook for another minute before adding cayenne and Worcestershire sauce.

Beat yolks lightly. Add a few tablespoons of white sauce to the yolks to warm them. Put sauce over low heat and pour in yolks in a thin stream, whisking. Add squash mixture and blend. Remove from heat. Set aside.

Beat whites until stiff. Fold into squash mixture with an over-and-under movement. Do not overmix. Pour mixture into soufflé dish and place in oven. Immediately lower heat to 375 degrees and bake for about 30 minutes, until puffy and golden.

Serve on a slick of sauce, and pass the remaining sauce.

Serves 6 to 8

FRESH TOMATO AND SWEET RED PEPPER SAUCE

The flavor of this sauce is dependent on the freshness of the tomatoes. If they are not vine ripened you should boost the sauce's flavor with a little tomato paste before continuing. Do this sparingly, however, tasting as you go along.

- ¼ cup olive oil
- ½ cup coarsely chopped onions
- 2 cups coarsely chopped sweet red peppers
- 2 teaspoons dried basil (optional)
- 2 tablespoons dry white wine
- 3½ cups peeled, seeded, and chopped ripe tomatoes

Heat the oil in a large skillet and add the onions, red peppers, and half the basil. Cook over medium heat for 10 minutes, stirring. Add the wine and reduce over medium-low heat for another 15 minutes, until thickened. Add tomatoes and remaining basil. Simmer for 25 minutes, stirring to prevent sticking, over medium-low heat. Purée in a food processor or blender until smooth.

This freezes very well and is reheatable in a microwave.

Makes about 3 cups

LEFT: **Yellow Squash Soufflé with Fresh Tomato and Sweet Red Pepper Sauce.**
ABOVE: **Potted clivia.**

PAN-SAUTÉED CATFISH FILLETS with PARSLEY-PECAN SAUCE

Many of the catfish you buy now are farm raised and seem to me to be somewhat sweeter than those we used to catch in the rivers and bayous. Maybe that is my imagination, but anyway I like farm-grown catfish better.

- **2 cups all-purpose flour**
- **1 tablespoon cayenne pepper**
- **1 tablespoon plus 1 teaspoon salt**
- **6 catfish fillets, about 5 to 6 ounces each**
- **2 or more tablespoons vegetable oil**
- **2 or more tablespoons unsalted butter**
- **2 cups Parsley-Pecan Sauce (recipe follows)**

Mix flour, cayenne, and salt (you can shake this in a bag). Spread it on a large platter and dredge each fillet, shaking off excess. Set aside on a sheet of waxed paper.

Heat half the oil and butter in a skillet large enough to accommodate 3 fillets at a time. When butter is foaming but not brown, add fillets and sauté on one side for about 4 minutes, until light golden. Turn fillets and spread the browned side with sauce; continue to sauté until underside is nicely browned, about another 4 minutes. Cover the skillet for a few minutes of the cooking time to melt the sauce. Remove fish to a platter.

Add the balance of the oil and butter and cook the remaining fillets. You may reheat these slightly under the broiler just before serving if you like.

Serves 6

PARSLEY-PECAN SAUCE

You might substitute pine nuts for the pecans, if you wish.

- **2 cups tightly packed fresh parsley, leaves and tender stems only**
- **½ cup olive oil**
- **½ cup broken pecan meats**
- **1 large clove garlic, cut into several pieces**
- **½ cup freshly grated Parmesan cheese**
- **½ cup freshly grated Romano cheese**
- **2 tablespoons unsalted butter, cut into pieces**
- **Salt**

Place parsley in a food processor and process until coarsely chopped, turning machine off and on and scraping down sides. Add all other ingredients except salt, and process until mixture makes a smooth paste. Correct seasoning with salt. Store, tightly covered, in the refrigerator.

This sauce freezes successfully. Allow to thaw in the refrigerator.

Makes about 2 cups

ABOVE: **Drawing room secretary.** RIGHT: **Pan Sautéed Catfish Fillets with Parsley-Pecan Sauce, and Lemon Carrots.** OPPOSITE: **View of the drawing room from the entrance hall.** OVERLEAF: **Flowers picked in the early morning.**

LEMON CARROTS

Sprinkle a little nutmeg on these if you choose.

2 **bunches small carrots, tops removed and scraped**

   Salt

   Juice of ½ large lemon, approximately

1 **tablespoon unsalted butter, approximately**

Cut the carrots into julienne strips, place in a saucepan, and cover with well-salted water. Boil, uncovered, for about 10 minutes, or until crisp-tender.

Drain and toss with the lemon juice and butter; if desired, add more of each to taste.

Serves 6

LEFT: **Hepplewhite windowseat.** ABOVE: **The drawing room.** TOP: **Detail of windowseat's embroidered fabric.** OPPOSITE TOP: **Painted detail on the windowseat.** OPPOSITE RIGHT: **Chess Pie with Blackberry Sauce.**

CHESS PIE
with BLACKBERRY SAUCE

This makes a very shallow pie, which is as it should be.

> **Dough for 1 pie crust (page 49)**
> 4 tablespoons (½ stick) unsalted butter
> ½ cup sugar
> 5 egg yolks
> 1 tablespoon flour
> 2 cups milk
> **Blackberry Sauce (recipe follows)**

Preheat the oven to 350 degrees. Roll dough out thin and use to line a 9-inch pie pan. Set aside.

Cream the butter and sugar together until light. Beat in yolks all at once. Mix in flour well. Stir in milk and mix well.

Pour into crust and bake about 1 hour, or until set and lightly browned.

Serve at room temperature with Blackberry Sauce.

Serves 6

BLACKBERRY SAUCE

When raspberries are in season, they make a very attractive sauce, too.

> **Approximately 2 cups (10 ounces) fresh or frozen blackberries**
> ¼ cup sugar
> 2 tablespoons freshly squeezed lemon juice
> 1 tablespoon dark rum

Combine the berries, sugar, and lemon juice in a small enameled saucepan. Simmer over low heat for about 15 minutes. Stir in rum.

Serve either hot or cold.

Makes about 1¾ cups

NOTE: If berries have not been frozen previously, you can freeze this sauce. Allow to thaw in the refrigerator.

Hunter's Buffet Supper at D'Evereux

D'EVEREUX, BUILT IN 1840, HAS A number of distinguishing architectural features aside from its gleaming two-story Doric columns. Among them is an unusual hipped roof topped with a cupola and a small cast-iron balcony, which was used in place of the more traditional second-story gallery.

The house was designed for William St. John Elliott of Maryland, a philanthropic Natchez planter, and named after Elliott's uncle, General John D'Evereux, who was honored for his superior service under Simón Bolívar in South America.

Inside, classic Greek motifs were used, the symbolism of which apparently appealed to the imagination of William Elliott, much as it did to many other local nineteenth-century country gentlemen: acanthus leaf for immortality, honeysuckle for hospitality, and the egg and dart for the infinite cycle of life. All of these appear carved in wood and plaster throughout the interior.

During its antebellum youth, D'Evereux was the setting for much spectacular entertaining, but perhaps its most renowned visitor was the charismatic Kentucky senator Henry Clay, who came to D'Evereux in December 1842. The U.S. presidential nominee was wined and dined luxuriously at an event that was later touted as the most magnificent gala the state of Mississippi had ever seen—it is said that 3,000 candles burned that evening. Apparently, Clay enjoyed his visit so much that he tarried long enough for his

portrait to be painted while relaxing in one of D'Evereux's parlors.

After Elliot's death in 1855, the estate passed through the hands of family members until its purchase in 1925 by Myra Virginia Smith of Chicago, who restored the house to its former splendor. Through

ABOVE: **Side window glimpsed through the foliage.** RIGHT: **Approach to D'Evereux.**

her efforts D'Evereux, long honored for its superb style and setting, became one of the jewels of the southland.

Many of the original exterior elements still remain, such as the almost 150-year-old bell that hangs at the rear of the house. Once used to awaken young boys at a nearby orphanage supported by Elliott, its toll also signaled work to begin in D'Evereux's vast vegetable gardens, the profits from which went to the maintenance of the orphanage. Also behind the main house are the original *garçonnière* and servants' quarters.

Inside, the parlors are furnished with much of the original furniture, including an early American Victorian parlor set, pier mirror, mahogany gaming table, and rare eighteenth-century tall case clock crafted by Englishman John Wyke of Liverpool.

Today, D'Evereux is owned and occupied by Mrs. T. B. Buckles and Mrs. and Mrs. Jack Benson, who have maintained and preserved the house for posterity.

D'Evereux is listed in the National Register of Historic Places and has been shown intermittently to tourists since 1932.

D. G.

M E N U

Onion Tart

Roast Venison with Hunter's Sauce

Scalloped Potatoes

Brussels Sprouts with Mustard

Sweet Potato Biscuits

Chocolate Pots de Crème

Wine · Coffee

THE MEAL MANY VISITORS HAVE remarked on D'Evereux's classic balance, but another aspect of this particular house that is not so immediately evident—certainly not judging from its magnificent façade—is its very manageable scale. Rooms are large with generous ceiling heights, but they are well proportioned, giving you the feeling of spaciousness without being cavernous, the way the imposing Stanton Hall is. This was a comfortable house, to be lived in.

The beautiful sideboard standing between the windows in the dining room presented an ideal spot from which to serve supper.

RIGHT: **Bisque nymph by A. Carrier, circa 1825.** OPPOSITE: **Onion Tart with garnishes.** OVERLEAF: **Sideboard set for the buffet supper.**

Almost everyone down here likes to hunt or knows someone who does, which means there is usually plenty of venison. Venison requires special care in its preparation. We made this a buffet supper because a leg of venison will easily serve a dozen people, and it is a perfect excuse to have a party.

But before the main course, to whet everyone's appetite, we had a luscious onion tart served with black olives, pickles, and peeled cherry tomatoes.

As accompaniments to the venison there were Brussels sprouts tossed in mustard butter and creamy scalloped potatoes. Scalloped potatoes is another of those dishes that can be made as simple or as complicated as you like. Substitutions for the light cream often used could be cottage cheese (plus a little milk), sour cream, or a combination of both with milk or cream. In this case, we made our scalloped potatoes with milk, topped with Swiss cheese—a very nice flavor balance for the roast.

There were also light sweet potato biscuits and butter.

Dessert was chocolate pots de crème. Not a bad way to start the fall.

ONION TART

Like most vegetable tarts, this also makes a nice luncheon dish. Just add a salad and some sherbet with cookies, and you have it done.

  2 tablespoons (¼ stick) unsalted butter
  4 cups thinly sliced sweet red onions
  ½ cup dry white wine
  ¼ cup minced fresh parsley
  1 prebaked tart shell (use half the pastry recipe on page 102)
  2 cups shredded Swiss cheese
    Black olives (optional)
    Pickles (optional)
    Peeled cherry tomatoes (optional)

Preheat the oven to 450 degrees. Melt the butter in a large skillet and add the onions. Sauté for 15 minutes over medium-low heat, until wilted. Add the wine and parsley, and simmer about 15 minutes more, until the liquid is almost evaporated. Layer 1½ cups cheese on the bottom of the tart shell and top with 1½ cups of onion mixture. Make another layer with the remaining cheese and then the onions. Place in the oven just long enough to melt the cheese. Don't overcook.

Garnish with black olives, pickles, and peeled cherry tomatoes.

Serves 8

SCALLOPED POTATOES

Everyone seems to love scalloped potatoes.

  6 cups thinly sliced boiling potatoes (⅛-inch slices)
  ½ small clove garlic
  4 tablespoons (½ stick) unsalted butter
  1 teaspoon salt
  ½ teaspoon freshly ground black pepper
  1½ cups grated Swiss or Gruyère cheese
  1 cup milk

Preheat the oven to 425 degrees. Keep potato slices in a bowl of cold water until ready to use.

Rub a 10-inch round baking dish that is 2 inches deep with the garlic and then generously grease. Drain and dry the potatoes. Layer them in the dish and divide the butter, salt, pepper, and cheese among layers, saving a layer of cheese for the top. Bring milk carefully to a boil and pour over all. Top with the last layer of cheese. Place in the oven and bake 30 minutes or more, until tender when pierced with the point of a knife and cheese is lightly browned.

Serves 8

ROAST VENISON with HUNTER'S SAUCE

This is a rare treat for me, although wild game seems to be finding its way into many restaurants these days.

- 12-pound leg of venison
- 4 cloves garlic, slivered
- 2 cups olive oil
- 4 cups red Burgundy wine
- 1 cup Worcestershire sauce
- 1 medium onion, sliced
- 5 tablespoons dried rosemary
- 2 tablespoons freshly ground black pepper
- Hunter's Sauce (recipe follows)

Wipe the meat with paper towels. Make deep incisions all over the roast and insert slivers of garlic. Reserve 1 cup of the olive oil, but combine all the other ingredients except sauce. Pour marinade over meat, cover, and refrigerate for 12 hours or overnight, turning every few hours.

Preheat the oven to 450 degrees. Place the venison leg in a roaster with about half the marinade. Pour remaining ½ cup of olive oil over. Bake for 15 minutes uncovered. Turn heat back to 250 degrees and insert a meat thermometer in the thickest part (do not let it touch the bone). Cover with foil and bake until thermometer reaches 150 degrees for medium (about 3 hours), or 165 degrees for well done. Baste often.

Allow roast to rest for 15 minutes before carving. Degrease the pan juices for the sauce. Serve with Hunter's Sauce.

Serves 12

HUNTER'S SAUCE

- 2 tablespoons unsalted butter
- 2 tablespoons chopped green onions, some tops
- 4 cups sliced mushrooms
- Salt
- ½ teaspoon freshly ground black pepper
- ⅔ cup dry white wine
- 1 cup degreased pan drippings
- 1 cup peeled, seeded, and chopped fresh tomatoes
- 1 teaspoon cornstarch mixed with 1 teaspoon water

In a large saucepan, melt the butter over medium heat and add the green onions, mushrooms, a pinch of salt, and the pepper. Sauté about 10 minutes, until vegetables are cooked. Add the wine and turn up the heat to high. Simmer briefly. Lower the heat to medium, add the pan drippings and tomatoes, and cook about 5 minutes. Do not overcook the tomatoes; they should still be slightly firm. Stir the cornstarch mixture into the sauce and cook 2 minutes, or until thickened. Serve hot.

Makes about 3½ to 4 cups

BRUSSELS SPROUTS with MUSTARD

Mustard is a perfect balance for the flavor of Brussels sprouts.

- 4 cups Brussels sprouts
- 5 cups salted water
- 2 tablespoons unsalted butter
- 2 tablespoons coarse-grained mustard
- ½ teaspoon freshly ground black pepper

Carefully wash the sprouts, trim the stems, and cut an *X* into the bottom of each with a sharp knife. Bring salted water to a boil and drop in sprouts. Boil about 15 minutes, until fork-tender. Drain well.

Melt the butter in a large skillet and stir in the mustard and pepper. Add the sprouts and toss to coat well. Add more salt and pepper, if desired.

Serves 8

SWEET POTATO
BISCUITS

*Here is a marvelous biscuit variation
you may never have had.*

- **2 cups mashed sweet potatoes**
- **2 cups all-purpose flour**
- **1 tablespoon unsalted butter**
- **1 tablespoon sugar**
- **1 teaspoon salt**
- **¼ teaspoon baking soda**
- **¼ to ½ cup buttermilk**

Preheat the oven to 400 degrees.
Grease 2 baking sheets.

Mix together thoroughly the sweet
potatoes, flour, butter, sugar, salt, and
baking soda. Mix in enough buttermilk to form a soft dough (it will be
sticky). Coat hands with flour and
lightly toss dough back and forth a
few times to cover with flour. Do not
overwork the dough. Roll out on a
well-floured board to a thickness of
½ inch. Cut with a floured ½-inch
biscuit cutter and bake for about 15
minutes, or until tops begin to slightly
brown.

Makes approximately 24

CHOCOLATE POTS
DE CRÈME

*This whole meal is fairly rich, so plan
on serving small portions of this dessert—as good as it is.*

- **¼ cup sugar**
- **2 cups light cream or
  half-and-half**
  Dash of salt
- **4 ounces sweet chocolate, grated**
- **4 ounces unsweetened
  chocolate, grated**
- **4 egg yolks**
- **1 teaspoon vanilla extract**
  **Flavored whipped cream
  (optional)**

Place sugar, cream, salt, and chocolates in the top of a double boiler and
melt over very low heat for 30 minutes, stirring often. Meanwhile, beat
yolks until thick and cream-colored.
Spoon a little of the chocolate mixture into the yolks and mix. While
beating, pour the balance of the chocolate mixture slowly into the yolks.
Return mixture to the double boiler
and cook another 30 minutes, stirring, or until thick. Stir in vanilla.

Pour ¼ cup of chocolate mixture
into each of 8 small *pots de crème*
cups. When slightly cool, cover and
refrigerate for 4 to 6 hours until firm.

Top each serving with a dab of flavored whipped cream.

Serves 8

ABOVE: **Chocolate Pots
de Crème.** OPPOSITE BELOW:
**Roast Venison and
Brussels Sprouts with
Mustard.** OPPOSITE TOP:
Garden steps. OPPOSITE
ABOVE: **Detail of
Steinway rococo piano
made in Hamburg,
1890.**

Dinner on the Gallery at the Elms

THE ELMS, SHELTERED INSIDE A haven of giant live oak trees in downtown Natchez, is an eclectic combination of three periods of early architecture and is one of Natchez's earliest documented antebellum houses. The original portion of the current two-and-a-half-story building, with its vernacular architecture and wide bannistered galleries, dates to 1804.

Its earliest owner was Scotsman John Henderson, who came to Natchez in 1787 and distinguished himself by writing the first book printed in the area. From Henderson, the Elms passed on to Lewis Evans, a well-known master builder and Mississippi territorial sheriff.

From 1825 to 1835, the Rev. and Mrs. George Potts made it Natchez's Presbyterian rectory and added the Elm's first wing, made distinct by high ceilings.

Again, the Elms expanded after the house was sold to David Stanton, brother of Frederick Stanton of nearby Belfast (which was later to be named Stanton Hall). In the 1850s, the Stantons added another two-story wing, this one Greek revival, leaving the house with unusual hallways connecting each section. One of these hallways enclosed an open cast-iron spiral staircase that was once used outside

After its newest addition, the front entrance faced away from its prior location overlooking the main dirt high-road linking Natchez and New Orleans.

The house passed to Mosely J. P. Drake in 1878, whose great-granddaughter, Alma Kellogg Carpenter, now lives there.

Much of the original Drake furniture, including a matching rococo revival parlor group with its original wool plush upholstery, is still in use. On the walls are ornamental shadow boxes of wax fruit and flowers, as well as framed embroideries made by Drake's daughters over the years. Morning-glory–patterned wall sconces and gasoliers are also still in place.

In florid prose typical of the day, the mid-nineteenth-century author Joseph Holt Ingraham observed in *South-West by a Yankee,* "Ambling along—to New Orleans we passed—the residence of the Presbyterian clergyman and one of the most charming retreats I have yet seen. Clumps of foliage, of the deepest green, were enameled with flowers of the brightest hues, and every tree was an aviary."

Surrounded by 114 acres when first built, the Elms now has retreated to three acres of camellias, azaleas, wisteria, and narcissus. Visitors can still sit in the garden's original white gazebo to watch family croquet games played on the lawn.

The Elms is listed in the National Register of Historic Places and has been shown to tourists since 1932.

D. G.

Garlic Smoked Tenderloin of Beef

Sweet Potato Chips

Caramelized Onions

Steamed Broccoli and Cauliflower

French Bread with Sweet Butter

Chocolate Cheesecake

Wine · Coffee

THE MEAL THE ELMS IS AN ECCENtric house by any standard. As you can see from the photographs, it is undeniably beautiful; but closer inspection reveals its many transformations. Over the years what began as a comparatively small house grew and sprawled out in all directions.

For instance, the present central hall of the Elms was the front of the house when it was first built; but when a new side was added to the front later, the entrance was changed, while the original façade windows were left in place. These now look from the hall into the dining room. Then there are steps up and steps down, inside and out, with rooms opening and closing unexpected into one another.

The Elms is a marvelous house that is fun to explore, filled with the personalities of its owners, past and present.

The upstairs gallery affords a restful view of the garden and brick boxwood-edged entrance walk below, all framed by the branches of great oak trees. What a spot to dine! We set up a table there to enjoy the sunset and a scrumptious meal, which was built around a garlic smoked tenderloin of beef.

The smoking of meats and fish of all sorts is quite popular in this area and it is often done in covered outdoor stoves. But of course, commercial smokers are avail-

able everyplace these days. One of the best things about smoked food is that it doesn't require much else to embellish the marvelous flavor, making it appealingly simple (when you have the equipment). So to go along with the meal we indulged in a little fancy by making wonderful orange-colored sweet potato chips and caramelized onions. The other vegetable dish was a combination I like, broccoli and cauliflower, steamed and tossed with butter—a dish as straightforward as the meat.

For dessert, we couldn't resist a recipe given to us for a sinful chocolate cheesecake. Or should I say blissfully sinful?

PRECEDING PAGE, LEFT: **Dinner on the upstairs gallery.** PRECEDING PAGE, RIGHT: **The Elms.** ABOVE: **Sheffield silver hunt cups.** ABOVE RIGHT: **Garlic Smoked Tenderloin of Beef, Sweet Potato Chips, Steamed Broccoli, and Caramelized Onions.**

GARLIC SMOKED TENDERLOIN OF BEEF

This recipe, or method, came to us from Barbara Rodriguez, who is noted for her smoked tenderloin in Natchez. Obviously, when you smoke meat you have to become familiar with the equipment you are using and make a few test runs with it first. Following are her comments.

5- **to 7-pound beef tenderloin, trimmed**

2 **large cloves garlic, crushed**

2 **tablespoons freshly ground black pepper**

1 **teaspoon salt**

Rub the meat with the crushed garlic, spreading it evenly on both sides, then do the same with the pepper and sprinkle with salt. Allow meat to absorb seasonings while preparing the fire.

"Build a fire with 5 pounds of charcoal in a small pit or 10 pounds of charcoal in a larger one. Allow your fire to burn off all starter fluid before putting meat on. When coals are white, close the pit to allow it to heat evenly. Adjust vents to begin smoking and allow fire to remain steady. Do not allow fire to flame. The meat should be about 1 foot from the coals or, if the pit is smaller, you may adjust the heat to a lower temperature to prevent meat from crusting. Cook meat for 15 minutes and turn. Cook for another 15 minutes. Each pit cooks differently, and you will be able to judge if the pit is cooking too fast and you need to adjust the heat accordingly. I do not use any type of wood for flavoring, just plain charcoal, but you could add wood chips if you like"—B. R.

I might add that one of those small thermometers which give instant readings when inserted in the meat would be useful here.

The above directions will produce a rare tenderloin. If you prefer medium, cook it for another 15 minutes. If you like it well done, you might as well eat pork. (For well done, cook for 1 hour, turning every 15 minutes.)

Serves 10 to 12

SWEET POTATO CHIPS

These come out a wonderful color and remain surprisingly crisp as they cool. The trick is not to try to fry too many at one time and to be sure the potatoes are sliced thin enough.

- 6 **medium sweet potatoes, peeled**
- 2 **to 3 quarts vegetable oil**
  Salt, sugar, and cayenne pepper

Slice the sweet potatoes as thin as possible. We used a small meat slicer, however a food processor fitted with the thinnest blade also works.

Immerse slices in cold water for about 10 minutes. Drain, pat with towels, and allow to dry. Heat the oil to 350 degrees in a large, deep pot or a deep-fat fryer. Use a candy thermometer to make sure the oil doesn't get too hot. Fry the chips a few at a time for 1¼ minutes, or until bright golden. Drain and sprinkle to taste with salt, sugar, and a dash of cayenne pepper.

Serves 6

STEAMED BROCCOLI AND CAULIFLOWER

We made this dish in a microwave oven the way we did the hot slaw at Dunleith. It cooked the vegetables perfectly and quickly. But you could also cook these quickly in a steamer, then toss them with the lemon juice, butter, salt, and pepper.

- 1 **head broccoli, flowerettes and tender stems only**
- 1 **head cauliflower, flowerettes only**
- 3 **tablespoons freshly squeezed lemon juice, about 1 large lemon**
- 1 **tablespoon unsalted butter, approximately**
- ½ **teaspoon salt**
- ½ **teaspoon freshly ground black pepper**

Combine the ingredients in a large glass bowl and cover tightly with plastic wrap. Make a steam vent in the plastic wrap using a fork or knife. Microwave on HIGH for 5 minutes. Toss and then give it 5 minutes more. Remove from oven and allow to stand, covered, for another few minutes. Correct seasoning and add more butter if you like.

Serves 6 or more

CARAMELIZED ONIONS

These are good served at room temperature.

- 4 **tablespoons (½ stick) unsalted butter**
- 5 **cups coarsely chopped onions**
- 1 **teaspoon red wine vinegar**
  Pinch of sugar
  Pinch of salt

Melt the butter over low heat in a large skillet. Add the onions and sauté for 20 minutes, moving them around constantly. Increase the heat to medium-high and brown onions stirring constantly, for another 10 minutes. Do not allow to burn. Stir in vinegar and seasonings.

Serves 6

CHOCOLATE CHEESECAKE

Anna Ernst, from the Parlor Restaurant in Natchez, passed this on to us. It's mighty good.

CRUST

- **3 cups chocolate wafer crumbs (do in food processor)**
- **⅓ cup (⅔ stick) margarine, melted**

FILLING

- **3 (8-ounce) packages cream cheese, at room temperature**
- **1 cup sugar**
- **4 eggs, at room temperatuare**
- **2 ounces semisweet chocolate, melted**
- **2 ounces sweet chocolate, melted**

To make crust, mix wafer crumbs and melted margarine with your hands until mixture holds together when pressed hard. Press into the bottom and half way up the sides of a 12-inch springform pan. You must press hard. Place in freezer until ready to fill.

Preheat the oven to 350 degrees. To make filling, cream the cheese at a low speed with a mixer for 2 minutes until free of lumps, scraping down sides of the bowl. Continue beating and add sugar in a steady stream. Cream at low speed for another minute, then beat on high for 30 seconds. Turn beater back to low and add the eggs, one at the time; beat until the shine leaves the batter before adding the next egg. Scrape down sides each time. Add chocolates and mix on low until well blended, about 40 seconds. Finally, turn mixer to high for another 40 seconds.

Pour batter into the prepared crust and bake for 40 minutes. The top will crack slightly when done. Turn off oven and open door; allow cake to cool in the oven. For best results, refrigerate overnight before cutting.

Serves 8 or more

OPPOSITE ABOVE: **Iron bench on the veranda.** OPPOSITE BELOW: **Blooming vine.** LEFT: **Hurricane lamp in the library.** BELOW: **Chocolate Cheesecake.**

Early Supper at Lansdowne

LANSDOWNE WAS BUILT IN 1852 as the centerpiece of a 600-acre wedding gift to Charlotte and George Marshall by the bride's father, "King" David Hunt, then one of the nation's wealthiest landholders.

A winding dirt road, sunken from decades of use, leads through a tangle of trees to this well-preserved structure, a living museum of mid-nineteenth-century architecture and interior detail.

Designed by the newlywed Marshalls and christened in honor of an English friend, the Marquis of Lansdowne, the house is only one story, though grand and generous inside. Originally intended to be two stories—a fact noticeable by its extended chimneys—the second floor was never added because of the financially devastating interruptions of the Civil War in 1861 and the depression of 1890 and 1929, which followed.

Lansdowne holds three large bedrooms to one side, and a large parlor, spacious dining room, and the original oak-cabineted kitchen to the other. A distinctive sixty-five foot foyer marks the center of the house and leads to the back courtyard, where two-story brick outbuildings accommodated servants and a billiard room was reserved for Lansdowne's gentlemen visitors.

The house overflows with original rosewood and mahogany furnishings, among them great oversize armoires. Other heirlooms include china, crystal, and miniature family portraits. Throughout are silver doorknobs, Aubusson rugs, and Egyptian marble mantels.

One such mantel forms the focus of the front parlor; carved in a calla lily design, it is reputed to be one of the finest in Natchez. The room's walls are still covered with the original wallpaper created by the noted nineteenth-century French designer Zuber. Until recently, the original window curtains and valances were still in use to shield the front rooms from damaging sunlight. However, these are now in museums and are replaced by exact copies.

Of particular interest is the house's great collection of fine silver, assembled over the generations by the Marshalls. The story is told that the family butler, fearing for the silver's safety, buried every piece in the cistern below the house after hearing news that nearby Vicksburg had fallen to Union soldiers. There the treasure remained until years later when it was unearthed, polished, and restored to its proper place in the house.

Another story has it that Charlotte Marshall was knocked down for standing her ground and refusing to give up her house to the Union soldiers who had demanded it. In spite, the men smashed Lansdowne's finest Parisian apricot china and sprinkled a trail of it on their way to Natchez. Miraculously, some of this china survived and is still in use today.

Its present owner, Mrs. John C. MacIlroy, came to Lansdowne as the bride of George M. Marshall III, almost sixty years ago. Today the house is occupied by Mr. and Mrs. MacIlroy; her daughter and son-in-law, Mr. and Mrs. Mackenzie Nobles; and the late Mr. Marshall's sister, Agnes Gardner. This noble house continues to shelter its family as it has always done.

Lansdowne, listed in the National Register of Historic Places, has been shown on Pilgrimage Tours since 1932.

D. G.

OPPOSITE ABOVE LEFT: **Gates at Lansdowne.** OPPOSITE BELOW LEFT: **Crossing the leafy gorge to Lansdowne.** OPPOSITE RIGHT: **The approach.** BELOW: **Decorative Captain's Walk.** BOTTOM: **Lansdowne.**

MENU

Gumbo Pot Pie
with Salt Corn Bread Crust

Green Pea and Dill Salad

Watermelon Rind Pickles

Pineapple-Lemon Mousse

Iced Tea or Wine · Coffee

THE MEAL LANSDOWNE, A COUNTRY house in the sense that it is situated in splendid isolation outside of the city limits, gives you an almost palpable sense of the past.

Approaching it through dense, cool trees, then crossing over a deep, mossy ravine spanned by a narrow iron bridge, one almost feels drawn backward in time. Maybe because Lansdowne is a house lived in and loved by the same family that built it, there is this feeling of closeness with an earlier period. I know the house must have its contented ghosts—such a lovely, quiet spot filled with memories.

Though Landsdowne displays its heritage with pride, it is by no means untouched by today—so an updated meal based on the past seemed right. We also wanted to make something easy to take outdoors, to be eaten in the approaching cool of the evening.

So, we took the ingredients for gumbo and made them into a pie with a corn bread crust—giving an old standby a new twist. Since pot pies are almost meals in themselves, all we added was a green pea salad laced with dill. And, of course, the ubiquitous sweet pickles.

For dessert we rather whimsically combined pineapple and lemon into a mousse.

Incidentally, in almost every place we dined in Natchez, we were offered a choice of wine or iced tea. That's what they do in trendy California food palaces. It's been done at Lansdowne that way for years.

PRECEDING PAGE: **Supper set out in the garden.** TOP: **Gumbo Pie with Salt Corn Bread Crust.** ABOVE: **18th-century French clock.**

GUMBO PIE with SALT CORN BREAD CRUST

FILLING

- ½ cup (1 stick) unsalted butter
- ½ cup all-purpose flour
- 2 large onions, coarsely chopped
- 2 green bell peppers, coarsely chopped
- 4 ribs celery, coarsely chopped
- 1 clove garlic, minced
- 4 cups hot chicken stock
- 2 cups fresh tomato purée
- 1 tablespoon chopped fresh parsley
- ½ teaspoon salt
- ½ teaspoon dried thyme
- 2 bay leaves
- ¼ teaspoon cayenne pepper
  Tabasco to taste (optional)
- 1 pound fresh okra, trimmed and cut into medium rings
- ½ pound link sausage, cut into rounds, cooked, and drained well
- 2 pounds shrimp, peeled and deveined

SALT CORN BREAD CRUST

- 1½ cups all-purpose flour
- ½ cup yellow cornmeal
- ¼ teaspoon salt
- ¾ cup (1½ sticks) unsalted butter, chilled and cut into small pieces
- 5 tablespoons ice water

To make the filling, melt the butter in a heavy pot over medium heat. Sprinkle in the flour when butter bubbles, then mix with a metal spatula, stirring and turning it over. (You are making a roux.) Watch this carefully as it starts to turn brown, because it will darken fast and you don't want to burn it. When the roux is a dark reddish tobacco color, about 5 minutes, quickly add the onions, peppers, celery, and garlic; mix. Mixture will sizzle and steam. Remove from stove for a bit, but continue to stir. Return to heat, then turn heat to low and continue to move vegetables around for about 5 minutes, until they wilt. Gradually stir in the chicken stock, then add the tomato purée, parsley, salt, thyme, bay leaves, cayenne, and Tabasco. Simmer, just bubbling, for 30 minutes. Add okra and sausage, and cook another hour until quite thick. (This may be made ahead of time up to this point and refrigerated. The crust should be made just before assembly.)

To make the crust, mix the flour, cornmeal, and salt in the bowl of a food processor fitted with a steel blade. Add the butter and process until mixture resembles coarse meal. With machine running, add the water. As soon as the dough begins to cling together, gather into a ball. Roll out dough into a circle large enough to top a large, deep 8-cup baking dish.

Preheat the oven to 400 degrees. To assemble the pie, fold the shrimp into the gumbo and top with the crust. Bake for 30 minutes, until top is golden. Serve in bowls.

Serves 6 or more

GREEN PEA AND DILL SALAD

You can stir a spoon or so of fresh mayonnaise into this just before it is served.

- 2 **12-ounce packages frozen green peas**
- 2 **tablespoons chopped fresh dill**
- 3 **tablespoons red wine vinegar**
- 2 **tablespoons olive oil**
  Salt and freshly ground black pepper
  Lettuce leaves

Place peas in a large pot and sprinkle with 1 tablespoon of the fresh dill. Pour hot water over them just to cover and blanch for about 7 minutes. Pour into a colander and rinse with cold water. When cool, mix peas with vinegar, oil, and the remaining dill. Marinate for several hours. Correct seasoning with salt and pepper (and more dill if you like).

Serve cold on lettuce leaves.

Serves 6

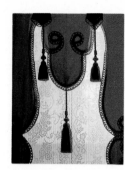

RIGHT: **Drawing room valance.** BELOW: **Detail of the marble fireplace.** BOTTOM: **Family miniatures.**

PINEAPPLE-LEMON MOUSSE

I like the way the flavors of pineapple and lemon complement each other.

- **2 cups finely chopped canned pineapple**
- **¼ cup freshly squeezed lemon juice**
- **1 cup water**
- **½ cup sugar**
- **1 envelope unflavored gelatin**
- **4 egg whites**
- **1 cup heavy cream**

Drain the pineapple. Slowly boil the lemon juice, ½ cup of the water, and the sugar about 5 minutes, until it makes a thin syrup. Mix the remaining ½ cup water with the gelatin. Whisk this into the hot syrup until completely dissolved. Cool mixture, then mix in pineapple.

Beat the egg whites until stiff, then fold into the pineapple mixture. Beat the cream over a bowl of ice until stiff, then fold in also. Turn mousse into a glass bowl and refrigerate for at least 6 hours.

Serves 6 to 8

WATERMELON RIND PICKLES

These are also wonderful with hot or cold ham or pork. This recipe comes to us from Laura Godfrey.

- **Rind of 1 large watermelon**
- **Pickling lime**
- **3½ pounds sugar**
- **2 cups distilled white vinegar**
- **1 ounce stick cinnamon**
- **1 ounce whole cloves**

Cut off the green skin and most of the pink meat (leave a tiny bit for color) from the watermelon rind. Cut rind into 1-inch cubes, cover with water, and mix in ½ ounce of lime for every gallon of rind. Soak overnight, then drain the rind but do not rinse.

In a large pot, cover rind with water again and cook over medium heat for about 1½ hours, or until rind can be pierced with a fork. Drain again. Mix the sugar, vinegar, cinnamon, and cloves, then cover the rind with this mixture and cook for 1 hour. While this is cooking, sterilize 6 pint jars and keep them hot. Place fruit in hot jars with a slotted spoon and then fill each jar with liquid. Leave spices in the liquid. Seal and process in a hot-water bath.

Makes 6 pints, depending on how much rind you have.

Wild Duck Dinner at Routhland

ROUTHLAND RISES AT THE CENter of ten acres of land granted to Job Routh by Baron Carondelet in 1792. The original house, once a cottage on the spacious grounds of what is now Dunleith, was completed very shortly after the property was acquired and is among the very earliest documented in the Natchez area.

By 1824, the cottage was being transformed into a substantial plantation house for Routh's son, John. With this initial expansion the house acquired its floor-to-ceiling windows that allow access to the gallery. Furnishings of polished walnut and cherry were added, as well as gold-leaf mirrors and cut-crystal chandeliers.

John Routh himself was extremely prosperous. He was described in a nineteenth-century publication as the world's most successful cotton planter, having shipped in one season alone as many as 4,000 bales to Europe. Good fortune flowed to both the younger and elder Routh until the Panic of 1837. With Routh's estate in disarray, he had to sacrifice the house at public auction to raise capital. Thereafter, it passed through a series of owners.

As the owners multiplied, so did the remodelings and alterations. Over the years, the original unassuming Federal house, composed of a large central hall connecting two rooms on either side, was made over a number of times to reflect the then-voguish styles.

Today the casement windows and portions of the large doors at each end of the hallway still contain the original white snowflake-patterned Bohemian glass. And the floors are still of the same sturdy random-width cypress boards.

Outside, curving front steps were added in the 1850s to add grace to the façade and as a symbol of hospitality. At the same time, marble mantels replaced the original wooden ones. Other changes included extensive additions at each end of the house, completed after 1871, when Routhland was the home of Mississippi's Civil War governor, Charles Clarke.

Finally, Routhland was acquired in 1944 by the late Laurie G. Ratcliffe and her children, Charles Everette Ratcliffe and Edna R. Howard. Mr. and Mrs. Charles Everette Ratcliffe, who still maintain the house, have done their share of renovating, happily continuing in the tradition of its previous owners.

The house, listed in the National Register of Historic Places, has been open to tourists since 1966.

D. G.

OPPOSITE: **Birdhouse designed to look like Routhland.** BELOW: **Routhland.**

MENU

Acorn Squash Soup

Wild Ducks Baked in Sauerkraut, with Duck-Leg Gravy

Wild Rice with Peppers

Glazed Carrots, Turnips, and Onions

Popovers

Warm Applesauce with Cream

Cinnamon-Pecan Squares

Wine · Coffee

ROUTHLAND IS ONE OF those Natchez houses that just grew. Much like the Elms in that respect, it spills all over the place with rooms entered through windows that once looked out onto the garden, and surprising wings that are almost complete houses in themselves.

It was built over many years, with the additions representing different periods of architecture and reflecting the ebb and flow of its original owners' fortunes.

Even with its many rooms and impressive façade, it is a country place at heart. So we felt Routhland would be perfect for a dinner centered around that staple of the fall Southern table, wild duck.

Dinner began with a creamy acorn squash soup, which calls for very little cream. But the main event was obviously the ducks. I think you will find this particular recipe interesting because it calls for cooking them in sauerkraut.

For those of you who don't know, wild ducks have a rather strong gamey flavor that needs to be tamed somewhat, and

this method, along with a bit of marinating, does the trick nicely.

Another favorite this time of the year is wild rice, here given an extra lift by the addition of peppers. It is very often an accompaniment to duck, no matter how it is prepared. And the combination of glazed root vegetables we chose is always popular, especially when the weather turns cool.

Finally, we figured a batch of popovers would be just right to complete this part of the meal.

The dessert, warm applesauce doused with heavy cream, has been a true plantation favorite for years. And truthfully it would have certainly been enough by itself —except that I had tasted some marvelous cookies flavored with bourbon.

Anyway, it was all delicious and brought back very happy memories of those fall days when my father used to come home from a hunting trip with a bag full of ducks. The only problem then, and now, is the buckshot, which can be rough on the teeth when you happen to bite down on one. Well, I guess that's a small price to pay for such a good dinner.

WILD RICE with PEPPERS

This dish will hold well while you get the rest of the dinner ready to serve. Place a tea towel over the pot and then replace the top. This keeps steam from collecting under the lid and dripping back into the finished rice.

- **1 cup wild rice**
- **2 cups chicken stock, heated to boiling**
- **1 tablespoon unsalted butter**
- **¼ cup finely chopped green bell peppers**
- **½ teaspoon salt**
- **1 teaspoon coarsely ground black pepper**

Place all ingredients in the top of a double boiler, cover, and cook over medium heat for 1 hour, or until liquid is absorbed and rice is fluffy. Fluff with a fork before serving.

Serves 6

ACORN SQUASH SOUP

You can substitute another type of squash or pumpkin for the acorn squash.

- **3 cups peeled, seeded, and coarsely chopped acorn squash**
- **½ cup finely chopped celery**
- **½ cup peeled and finely chopped apples**
- **1 cup peeled and coarsely chopped potatoes**
- **½ cup coarsely chopped onions**
- **½ cup scraped and coarsely chopped carrots**
- **¼ teaspoon dried oregano**
- **½ teaspoon dried rosemary**
- **5 cups chicken stock**
- **¼ cup heavy cream (optional)**
  Salt and freshly ground black pepper

Combine all the ingredients except the cream in a large saucepan. Simmer over medium heat for 30 minutes, stirring occasionally to keep from scorching, until vegetables are soft. Purée the mixture in a food processor until very smooth. Return to pot and stir in cream over medium heat until heated thoroughly. Do not allow to boil. Correct the seasoning with salt and a dash of pepper if necessary.

Serves 6 to 8

WILD DUCKS BAKED IN SAUERKRAUT, with DUCK-LEG GRAVY

As I said in my introduction, it is very important to marinate wild ducks before baking. Some people simply use a solution of half water and half vinegar.

4 (2- to 2½-pound) wild ducks

4 cups vinegar (any type)

5 cups dry red wine

4 cups water

10 sprigs fresh thyme, crushed

2 teaspoons dried thyme

2 teaspoons dried sage

2 teaspoons freshly ground black pepper

1 teaspoon salt, plus additional to taste

2 tablespoons vegetable oil

6 cups sauerkraut

1 cup chopped green onions, some tops

1 cup chopped celery

1 cup chopped green bell peppers

1 cup peeled, seeded, and chopped tomatoes

4 cloves garlic

Tabasco

Make sure the ducks are very clean—wash them thoroughly and pat dry.

Combine the vinegar, 4 cups wine, water, and fresh thyme in a large container and marinate the ducks in this. Refrigerate overnight. The acid in the marinade will draw out the blood.

Remove the ducks from the marinade and discard liquid. Separate the duck legs from the breast by pressing them down and outward so that they break at the joint. Make an incision between the breast and the leg, and cut through the back. Set legs aside.

Preheat the oven to 350 degrees. Season the breasts with the dried thyme, sage, pepper, and salt. In a large skillet, heat the oil over medium heat and brown the birds evenly on all sides. Remove from skillet, set aside, and discard oil.

GLAZED CARROTS, TURNIPS, AND ONIONS

You can add rutabagas to this combination if you like.

1½ cups scraped carrots, cut into medium rings
1½ cups peeled and cubed white turnips (½-inch cubes)
1½ cups very small peeled white onions (see Note)
2 cups water
½ teaspoon salt
3 tablespoons unsalted butter
¼ cup honey
2 tablespoons freshly squeezed lemon juice

Place the vegetables in a saucepan with the water and salt. Simmer about 20 minutes, just until fork-tender. Meanwhile, simmer the butter, honey, and lemon juice in a small saucepan for 10 or 15 minutes, until slightly reduced. Drain vegetables well. Toss with glaze before serving.

Serves 6 to 8

NOTE: If you drop onions in a pot of boiling water for about a minute, their skins will slip right off.

POPOVERS

I sometimes substitute a half-and-half mixture of finely chopped nuts and flour for the flour measure in popover recipes.

1 cup milk
1 tablespoon unsalted butter, melted
1 cup all-purpose flour
¼ teaspoon salt
2 eggs, lightly beaten

Preheat the oven to 475 degrees. Grease 2 standard-size muffin tins and set aside.

Beat the milk, butter, flour, and salt together until smooth; it will be the consistency of heavy cream. Add the eggs, one at a time, mixing after each, but do not overbeat. Fill the tins three-fourths full and bake for 15 minutes. Lower the heat to 350 degrees and bake another 20 minutes. Do not peek. They should be nicely browned and pulling away from the sides.

Makes 9 or more

Stuff each duck with about 1½ cups of sauerkraut and place in a roaster. The sauerkraut will draw out the wild flavor and keep the ducks moist without affecting the taste.

Place the duck legs, vegetables, garlic, and remaining 1 cup wine in a baking dish. Bake along with ducks in the oven for about 1½ to 2 hours (2 hours will yield well-done ducks). Remove the ducks from the oven and discard the sauerkraut. Remove the duck legs from the vegetables, purée the sauce, and add Tabasco and additional salt to taste.

Slice the duck, top the slices with gravy, and give everyone a leg.

Serves 6 to 8

OPPOSITE: **Wild Ducks Baked in Sauerkraut; Wild Rice with Peppers; Glazed Carrots, Turnips, and Onions; and Popovers.** TOP: **Silver Chantilly goblets.** ABOVE: **Garden swing.**

LEFT: **Rocking chairs on the veranda.** OPPOSITE: **Magnolia blossom.** BELOW: **Cinnamon-Pecan Squares and Warm Applesauce with Cream.**

WARM APPLESAUCE with CREAM

If you are pressed for time, substitute a good commercial applesauce.

- **4 cups peeled, cored, and coarsely chopped tart apples**
- **2 cups water**
- **½ cup honey**
- **1½ teaspoons vanilla extract or bourbon**
- **1 cup heavy cream (or more)**

In a large saucepan over low heat, cook the apples and water for about 15 to 20 minutes, or until they are soft. Purée in a food processor and return to the pan. Add the honey and vanilla or bourbon. Simmer for another 30 minutes until liquid is reduced.

Serve this warm with cold heavy cream.

Makes approximately 3½ cups

NOTE: If you use commercial unsweetened applesauce, mix it with honey and vanilla and simmer for 30 minutes.

CINNAMON-PECAN SQUARES

This recipe came from Edna Howard.

- ½ **cup (1 stick) unsalted butter, softened**
- 1¼ **cups sugar**
- 2 **cups all-purpose flour**
- ½ **teaspoon salt**
- 1 **egg, separated**
- 2 **tablespoons bourbon**
- 2 **teaspoons ground cinnamon**
- 1½ **cups coarsely chopped pecans**

Preheat the oven to 250 degrees. Grease two 10 × 15-inch jelly-roll pans. Cream the butter and 1 cup of the sugar with your hands. (Ms. Howard says a mixer incorporates too much air.) Sift the flour, add salt, and sift again. Stir the egg yolk into the creamed mixture, then add half the flour and 1 tablespoon of the bourbon. Mix well and add remaining flour and bourbon; mix well again.

Divide dough in half and spread on jelly-roll pans with a spatula. Pat down with hands. Pour half an egg white on each spread of cookie dough, and tilt and rock pans until white coats the top. Pour off excess.

Mix the remaining ¼ cup sugar with the cinnamon and sprinkle evenly over both pans. Sprinkle pecans over all as well, pressing very lightly. Bake for 1 hour. Cut into 2 × 3-inch bars while hot and allow to cool in pans.

Incidentally, these freeze well.

Makes approximately 60

Festive Supper at Twin Oaks

❧

T WIN OAKS IS ELEGANT YET unpretentious, and it epitomizes antebellum architectural sophistication. The early urban cottage, sheltered by now-ancient live oaks, overlooks Homochitto Street, once a major regional thoroughfare linking Natchez to New Orleans.

At one time Twin Oaks shared the same Spanish land grant as nearby Dunleith, though their similarities are only in proximity. Whereas its neighbor is surrounded on all four sides by soaring columns, Twin Oaks is a one-and-a-half-story white painted brick house entered through a Greek revival portico composed of four thick Doric columns supporting a classic pediment.

The oldest section of the house, now the dining room wing, was built between 1810 and 1814 by Lewis Evans, a wealthy planter and influential terrorial sheriff. By 1823, however, the house belonged to Pierce and Cornelia Connelly, whose lives, more than any of its other owners, were to take the most radical and unexpected turns.

The Connellys had moved to Natchez from Pennsylvania to work in the Trinity Episcopal Church, and they had bought Twin Oaks from the widow of Dr. Josiah Morris. (Incidentally, Dr. Morris was to be the first of three medical doctors to occupy the house.) It was during this time that the front addition was probably con-structed and the house given the name "White Cottage"—a title it would carry for the next 100 years.

In 1835, the Connellys converted to Catholicism, left Natchez, and moved to Rome. Pierce Connelly eventually became a priest and Cornelia, a nun. Cornelia later was sent by the pope to England, where she founded the Society of the Holy Child Jesus for young nuns. Today she is nominated for sainthood, and a small chapel behind Twin Oaks is dedicated to her memory.

During the tumultuous 1860s, Twin Oaks survived Union troops that took over the house during their stay in Natchez. After the Civil War, the property saw a series of ownership changes until 1940, when it was purchased by its present residents, Dr. and Mrs. Homer A. Whittington, who are devotedly involved with the Natchez Pilgrimage.

The Whittingtons renamed their home Twin Oaks, inspired by the matching pair of towering antebellum oaks that mark its entrance, and set about the job of restoration. One of the accidental discoveries during this renovation was that all of the house's hardware is of Sheffield silver.

After finishing the interior, the back gallery was enclosed and extended to provide a family room and a passage to the older dining room wing.

Twin Oaks has been shown to tourists since 1941, and is listed in the National Register of Historic Places.

D. G.

MENU

Mushroom Consommé

Poached Spinach-Wrapped Oysters

Dirty Rice

Buttered Acorn Squash

Crescent Rolls

Sherry Spice Cake with Brown Sugar Glaze

Wine · Coffee

THE MEAL TWIN OAKS, ALTHOUGH changed and added to over the years, and approached from the street by an imposing number of steps, still retains that very appealing quality of a cottage—especially when compared to its close neighbor, Dunleith. It's a peaceful spot, a place where you can imagine the family gathered in the evenings listening to music or quietly reading. And yet Twin Oaks also has the rather serene and sophisticated air of a city house. It's the best of both worlds.

This combination led us to devise a festive sort of city-country supper menu. The whole meal was delightfully light, even with the spice cake dessert.

And the beautifully scaled dining room,

housed in its own separate wing and opening onto a small, private side gallery, proved the perfect setting to serve the meal.

We started with a very flavorful mushroom consommé, which was followed by delicate spinach-wrapped oysters quickly poached—that's the city part of the menu.

The stylish oysters were served on a bed of dirty rice. For the uninitiated, dirty rice is rice that is combined with puréed chicken livers and vegetables—a country dish if there ever was one. Actually I grew up on dirty rice, but I had forgotten how truly delicious it is. I think you will make it often once you have tried it.

All this was accompanied by buttered acorn squash and crescent rolls.

Now for the dessert. In these parts there must be as many variations of spice cake with a brown sugar glaze as there are recipes for bread pudding in New Orleans. But it is so satisfying that I never tire of it. Like most people who have Southern backgrounds, I have a real weakness for cakes—and pies.

Incidentally, from a practical standpoint, spice cakes tend to be more flavorful the day after they are baked, if there is any left.

PRECEDING PAGE, LEFT: **Twin Oaks.** PRECEDING PAGE, RIGHT: **Mushroom Consommé and Crescent Rolls.**

MUSHROOM CONSOMMÉ

This has a very gentle flavor.

- 6 cups clarified chicken stock
- 1 cup dry white wine
- 1 teaspoon dried tarragon
- ½ teaspoon salt
- 2 tablespoons unsalted butter
- 3 cups thinly sliced fresh mushrooms

In a large saucepan, combine the stock, wine, tarragon, and salt. Simmer for about 30 minutes to reduce and intensify the flavor. Melt the butter in a medium skillet over medium heat. Add the mushrooms and sauté 2 to 3 minutes, until they begin releasing their liquid.

To serve, combine mushrooms with the stock and reheat.

Serves 8 or more

POACHED SPINACH-WRAPPED OYSTERS

The flavor of spinach is delicious with oysters.

- 40 large shucked oysters, with liquor
- 1 cup dry white wine
- 1 cup water
- ½ teaspoon dried thyme
- ½ teaspoon salt, or more to taste
- 2 tablespoons chopped green onions, some tops
- ½ cup (1 stick) butter
- 1 cup peeled and seeded tomatoes
   Freshly ground black pepper (optional)
- 40 young spinach leaves, stemmed and washed

Drain the oysters and reserve 2 cups of their liquor. Place oysters and liquor, along with the wine, water, and thyme, in a small saucepan. Bring to just simmering over medium heat, then poach oysters for about 1½ minutes, until the edges curl. Remove with a slotted spoon and set aside. Add the green onions to the poaching liquid and reduce over medium-high heat for about 30 minutes. Whisk in the butter by tablespoons. Add the tomatoes. Add more salt and some pepper, if desired. This should retain a fresh, light taste. Set aside.

Preheat the oven to 350 degrees. Bring several cups of water to a boil in a large saucepan and blanch the spinach leaves for 45 seconds. Remove and dry. Roll each oyster in a spinach leaf and place them together in single layer in a greased 10-inch baking dish. Pour the reduced oyster liquid over all and place in oven for about 7 minutes, until heated through. Do not overcook; this is only to reheat. Serve over Dirty Rice (recipe follows), with sauce spooned over all.

Serves 8

OPPOSITE: **Side gallery detail.** ABOVE: **Poached Spinach-Wrapped Oysters, Dirty Rice, and Buttered Acorn Squash.**

CRESCENT ROLLS

These smell marvelous while they are baking.

- 1 **package active dry yeast**
- ¼ **cup warm water (about 110 degrees)**
- 4½ **cups all-purpose flour**
- ½ **cup sugar**
- 1 **teaspoon salt**
- ¾ **cup (1½ sticks) unsalted butter, softened**
- 2 **eggs, lightly beaten**
- ¾ **cup warm milk (about 110 degrees)**
  Melted butter, for brushing rolls

Dissolve yeast in the warm water; let stand for 5 minutes, covered with a tea towel. Meanwhile, combine the flour, sugar, and salt in a food processor by pulsing several times. Add butter to the flour and process until mixture resembles coarse meal. In a separate bowl, combine eggs, milk, and yeast mixture. Add to the flour and process until dough forms a ball. Place in a lightly buttered bowl, cover, and refrigerate overnight.

Punch dough down and divide in half. Roll each half into a 12-inch circle at least ¼ inch thick. Cut each circle into 12 pie-shape wedges. Roll up each wedge tightly, begining at the wide end. Seal the point with a little ice water, pressing down lightly. Place on greased baking sheets, point sides down, and curve into a crescent shape. Brush each with a little melted butter. Cover rolls and allow to rise in a warm place (80 degrees) for about 1 hour.

Preheat the oven to 400 degrees.

Bake rolls for 8 to 10 minutes, until golden.

Makes 24

DIRTY RICE

Dirty rice is about as Southern a dish as there is.

- ½ **pound chicken livers**
- 1 **medium onion, very coarsely chopped**
- 3 **ribs celery, very coarsely chopped**
- 1 **medium green bell pepper, very coarsely chopped**
- 3 **fresh medium tomatoes, very coarsely chopped**
- 1 **cup very coarsely chopped fresh parsley**
- 4 **tablespoons (½ stick) unsalted butter**
- ½ **teaspoon salt**
- ½ **teaspoon freshly ground black pepper**
- ½ **teaspoon dried thyme**
- 1 **large bay leaf**
- 2 **cups long-grain rice (not instant)**
- 4 **cups chicken stock, heated to boiling**

In a food processor fitted with a steel blade, purée the livers, onion, celery, green pepper, tomatoes and parsley. Melt the butter in a large heavy saucepan, and add purée, salt, pepper, thyme, and bay leaf. Cook, stirring often, over medium-low heat for 30 minutes. Add the rice and sauté over medium heat for 2 minutes, stirring with a fork. Add boiling stock, stir, and cover. Cook over low heat for 15 minutes, then remove from heat and allow rice to steam, covered, for 20 minutes. Fluff with a fork and adjust seasoning if necessary.

Serves 8

BUTTERED ACORN SQUASH

The touch of nutmeg in this recipe piques the flavor of the squash very nicely. You can add more butter if you like.

- 1 acorn squash, about 1 pound
- ¼ teaspoon grated nutmeg, or more to taste
- ½ teaspoon salt
- 2 tablespoons unsalted butter

Cut the squash into medium-thick slices, about ¼ inch or more. Discard seeds and stem. Peel with a very sharp paring knife—acorn squash is hard. Place slices in a steamer, cover, and cook about 20 minutes, until fork-tender. While still hot, sprinkle with nutmeg and salt. Toss with the butter.

Serves 8

NOTE: As an alternate method, split and bake lightly buttered halves until fork tender, scoop out pulp, and mash with butter and nutmeg.

SHERRY SPICE CAKE with BROWN SUGAR GLAZE

Now that I think of it, spice cakes, while they are baking, smell just as good in their own way as rolls do when they are in the oven.

CAKE

- 2⅓ cups sifted cake flour
- 1½ teaspoons baking powder
- ½ teaspoon baking soda
- 1 teaspoon grated nutmeg
- 1 teaspoon ground cinnamon
- ½ teaspoon ground cloves
- ½ teaspoon salt
- 1½ cups granulated sugar
- ¾ cup (1½ sticks) unsalted butter
- 3 eggs, separated
- ½ cup plus 1 tablespoon buttermilk
- ¼ cup dry sherry

BROWN SUGAR GLAZE

- 2 cups firmly packed light brown sugar
- ¾ cup heavy cream
- 4 tablespoons (½ stick) unsalted butter
- 1 teaspoon vanilla extract
- 1 cup confectioners' sugar

Preheat the oven to 350 degrees. Lightly grease and flour a 9 × 5-inch loaf pan or tube pan. Set aside.

To make the cake, sift together the flour, baking powder, baking soda, nutmeg, cinnamon, cloves, and salt onto a sheet of waxed paper. Set aside. Sift the granulated sugar into a bowl with the butter. Cream together until very light and fluffy, about 3 minutes. Beat in egg yolks one at a time. Combine buttermilk and sherry, then add to creamed mixture, alternating with the flour mixture. Beat egg whites until stiff and fold into batter. Pour into prepared pan and bake about 1 hour, or until a cake tester comes out clean.

To make glaze, place the brown sugar, cream, and butter in a saucepan and bring slowly to a rolling boil, stirring all the while. Remove from heat and stir in vanilla and then confectioners' sugar. Pour over top of cake and allow to run down the sides naturally. Do not try to spread.

Serves 12

Fall Supper
at Linden

LINDEN'S CONSTRUCTION BEGAN as early as 1792, making it one of the oldest surviving Natchez houses. The property on which it was built, in common with many other eighteenth-century land acquisitions, originated as a Spanish land grant, this one to a Madam Sara Truly. She sold the property to Alexander Moore, a Natchez real estate magnate, who left it to his son, James.

James Moore succeeded in building a house on the property that was as grand, or grander, than most in the township. The house was made of native cypress and had a ninety-eight-foot gallery spanning its entire front façade. Not only could it be entered through its large polished front door but also through the jib windows that marched across the whole width of the house.

Side wings were added in 1818 by Thomas B. Reed, the first U.S. Senator from the new state of Mississippi. He christened the house Reedland. Reed also added the beautiful main doorway crowned by a fine Adam fan light with richly detailed diamond and oval sidelights.

By 1829, Linden—as the house was called by its newest occupant, John Kerr —was double its original size. Even though the linden tree does grow in the South, it is said that Kerr, of German descent, named the house after the national tree of his family's native country.

Finally, by 1840, a widow, Jane Gustine Conner, had acquired Linden and had added its two rear wings with a bricked courtyard for entertaining. And entertain she did, with a house full of servants and thirteen children. During the Civil War, Jane Conner came to be known affectionately as the "Little War Mother," having sent five of her sons and seven of her sons-in-law to fight for the Confederacy.

Today, the sixth generation of Conners lives at Linden and still uses many of the family furnishings from the early 1800s. Among these is a New York Hepplewhite banquet table in the dining room with the original white painted cypress punka suspended over it.

Many of Linden's mantelpieces are in the Federal style, with some in the older parts of the house even simpler. Recently, family members replaced several marble mantels in this old section with the originals. And after lifting off eight coats of paint from these original mantels, it was discovered that there was a black coat on each. It had been applied in 1799, when it was the custom to darken mantels and doors as a gesture of respect for George Washington, who died that year.

Linden is now owned by Mrs. Richard Conner Feltus. It has been shown intermittently to Natchez tourists since 1932, and is listed in the National Register of Historic Places.

D. G.

Corn and Oyster Chowder

Roast Loin of Pork with Natural Gravy

Spiced Sweet Potatoes

Creamy Spinach

French Bread Rolls

Almond-Pear Torte

Wine · Coffee

THE MEAL LINDEN, WITH ITS BROAD front gallery and two long back wings, contains many rooms. But unlike some of the neighboring plantations, which were seemingly enlarged and expanded in a rather casual way, this place was obviously very carefully planned early on to accommodate an extended family. As a matter of fact, I remarked on the number of bedrooms I was walking through—nine in all—on my very first visit. It doesn't take much imagination to appreciate what was involved in preparing the daily meals for such an extensive establishment. Interestingly, though, Linden isn't grand or palatial in scale, but very human.

Seeing the house today, one can't help but wonder what it must have been like when it was running full tilt, filled with family members, guests, and servants. Probably quite a jolly place.

The meal we had in Linden's understandably generous dining room started with a smooth corn and oyster chowder. Here are two ingredients that were made for one another; their flavors couldn't be more suited.

Then after soup, we had that Southern favorite—pork—roasted this time around and served with natural gravy (the pan juices). Actually, most people in these parts like pork about any way it's prepared. Can't say I blame them on that score. I'm pretty partial to it myself.

To accompany the roast were spiced sweet potatoes, another perfect combination.

And for balance there was creamed spinach. This particular recipe in which banana is used to give the mixture a creamy texture instead of the more usual heavy cream—was a pleasant variation.

As you must have noticed by now, rolls of all sorts are popular with meals, so we served yet another kind.

For dessert, we made a simple pear torte. Although the torte looks substantial, it is really very light and is a nice ending to this fairly hearty meal.

CORN AND OYSTER CHOWDER

Some people add a little diced sweet red pepper to this, but I like it best as is.

½ cup (1 stick) unsalted butter
1 cup finely chopped onions
1 cup finely chopped celery
2 cups cubed potatoes (½-inch cubes)
2 cups chicken stock
2 cups water
½ teaspoon dried basil
¼ teaspoon salt
3 tablespoons flour
2 cups milk
1 (20-ounce) can whole kernel corn, drained, or about 2 cups fresh or frozen corn
20 medium oysters, shucked with 2 tablespoons oyster liquor

In a large pot, melt the butter over medium heat and add the onions and celery. Sauté about 10 minutes, until slightly browned. Add the potatoes, stock, water, basil, and salt. Simmer over low heat for 30 to 45 minutes, until potatoes are tender and falling apart.

In a small saucepan, whisk together the flour and ½ cup of the milk. Bring this to boiling over low heat and whisk into the simmering stock. Add the remainder of the milk and the corn. Heat, but do not boil, the soup over low heat for another few minutes.

Just before serving, add oysters and liquor. Heat about 5 to 6 minutes, until oysters puff up and edges are curly.

Serves 8 to 10

PRECEDING SPREAD, LEFT: **Afternoon sun in the library.** PRECEDING SPREAD, RIGHT: **Linden.** OPPOSITE: **Baltimore desk in the library, circa 1800.** ABOVE: **Corn and Oyster Chowder.** LEFT: **View of the dining room.**

SPICED SWEET POTATOES

Light brown sugar can be substituted for the honey, if you like.

6 medium sweet potatoes, boiled, peeled, and cut into ½-inch-thick slices

½ teaspoon ground cinnamon

½ teaspoon ground ginger

½ teaspoon grated nutmeg

½ teaspoon ground cloves

½ teaspoon salt

4 tablespoons (½ stick) unsalted butter, cut in pieces

3 tablespoons honey

Preheat the oven to 375 degrees. Butter a 10-inch round baking dish, that is 2 inches deep.

Set out sweet potatoes. Combine the spices and salt. Layer the potatoes in the dish, sprinkling each layer with some of the spice mixture, dotting with butter, and drizzling with honey. Bake, uncovered, for 20 minutes, until heated and ingredients are well combined.

Serves 8 to 10

ROAST LOIN OF PORK with NATURAL GRAVY

You may dredge the pork in flour mixed with herbs, shaking off the excess; this gives it a crustier surface.

- 4- to 5-pound boned loin of pork
- 1 teaspoon salt
- 1 teaspoon freshly ground black pepper
- 1 teaspoon dried thyme
- 1 teaspoon paprika
- ½ teaspoon mace
- ¼ teaspoon ground cumin
- 1 medium onion, thinly sliced

Preheat the oven to 450 degrees. Mix the salt, pepper, thyme, and spices. Sprinkle evenly on all sides of roast. Place onion slices in the bottom of a roasting pan and put roast, fat side up, on them. Insert a meat thermometer. Sear in the hot oven for 15 minutes, then turn heat down to 325 degrees. Bake for 1 hour, cover with foil, and bake another 45 minutes to an hour, until internal temperature is 160 degrees.

Serves 8 to 10

OPPOSITE: **Looking down into the courtyard.** ABOVE: **Adam mantel in the bedroom.** RIGHT: **Roast Loin of Pork with Natural Gravy, Spiced Sweet Potatoes, Creamy Spinach, and French Bread.**

CREAMY SPINACH

Poached pears are also quite good puréed with spinach.

- 4 pounds fresh spinach, carefully washed and stemmed
- 1½ cups sliced bananas
- 2 teaspoons freshly squeezed lemon juice
  Salt and freshly ground black pepper

Place the undrained spinach in a deep pot. Cook over high heat, shaking pan. Stir and fold spinach once, mashing down as it wilts, and cook about 4 minutes, until tender. Remove to a colander and press with the back of a wooden spoon to get rid of excess moisture. Place spinach and other ingredients in a food processor and purée until mixture is creamy.

Serves 8

FRENCH BREAD
ROLLS

All of the dough folding required here is typical of some French breads, but it isn't really as complicated as it may sound.

1½ **envelopes active dry yeast**

1¼ **cups warm water (about 110 degrees)**

2 **tablespoons unsalted butter**

3½ **cups all-purpose flour**

1 **teaspoon salt**

Blend the yeast with ¼ cup of the warm water. Set aside. Heat the balance of the water and butter together in a small saucepan until butter melts. Set aside to cool slightly. Meanwhile, place flour and salt into a food processor and mix by pulsing a few times. Add the dissolved yeast and the butter mixture. Process until dough forms a ball.

On a lightly floured surface, knead dough for several minutes, then place in a lightly buttered, straight-sided bowl. Cover with a tea towel and allow to rise for 1 hour in a warm spot until doubled in bulk.

Turn out dough onto a floured surface and knead gently a few minutes. Return to the bowl and allow to

rise again, for 1 hour, or until doubled in bulk.

Punch dough down and turn out once more, dividing into 10 equal balls. Flatten each ball to make a circle about ¼ inch thick. Fold one side of the circle about two-thirds of the way over the other side. Give the folded dough a quarter turn and fold *that* side two-thirds of the way over the opposite side. Repeat until you have gone all the way around and have a small, fat circle of dough. Place folded side down on a baking sheet. Repeat with other circles, placing them several inches apart on the sheet. Handle dough quickly and lightly. Cover and allow these to rise for 1½ hours.

Preheat the oven to 450 degrees. Place rolls in the oven and, after a minute, toss 4 or 5 ice cubes onto the bottom of the oven to give you a bit of steam. After another 5 minutes, toss in another 4 ice cubes. Bake for another 10 minutes, then turn heat back to 400 degrees and bake for an additional 20 minutes, until tops are golden.

Makes 10 small loaves

ALMOND-PEAR
TORTE

You can actually use any kind of nuts, or a combination. Each has its own distinctive taste.

2 to 3 **pears, cut into ⅛-inch slices**

1 **cup water mixed with 2 tablespoons freshly squeezed lemon juice**

1 **cup sugar**

6 **eggs, separated**

1 **cup finely ground blanched almonds**

½ **cup lightly toasted fine white bread crumbs**

½ **teaspoon vanilla extract**

½ **cup apple jelly, melted**

Soak the pear slices in the lemon water to keep them from turning brown.

Preheat the oven to 350 degrees. Lightly grease the bottom of an 8-inch springform cake pan. Sift the sugar into a large bowl and cream with the egg yolks until light in color, about 3 or 4 minutes. Stir in the almonds, bread crumbs, and vanilla. Mix well. Beat the egg whites until stiff, then fold lightly into the batter.

Pour batter into pan and bake for 40 minutes, or until cake tester comes out clean. Cool in pan before removing. Drain the pear slices thoroughly, then arrange on top of the torte. Glaze with melted jelly.

Serve with ice cream or whipped cream.

Serves 8 to 10

LEFT: **Detail of an Aubusson carpet in the living room.** OPPOSITE: **Almond-Pear Torte.**

Natchez Desserts

I DON'T SUPPOSE IT'S ANY NEWS that Southerners have a real weakness for sweets. Maybe it was all that sugarcane everyplace. Whatever, over the years this region has come up with some truly winning desserts that are generally simple and straightforward—just the sort of thing I like.

Anyway, when I started working with Courtney Parker, a young Southern belle and an impressive cook, on the recipes and menus you see in this book, she kept telling me about desserts and treats that sounded so mouthwatering we simply had to try them. The only problem was that finally there were more desserts than meals.

So here is a collection of desserts Courtney culled from family and friends —and a couple she invented herself—that didn't find their way into the menus.

You'll love them, as I did.

ABOVE: **Clara Nell Adams White Chocolate Cake.**
OPPOSITE: **Plum Tart.**

PLUM TART

Other kinds of fruit, such as peaches, can also be used.

SWEET PASTRY CRUST

- 1½ cups all-purpose flour
- 3 tablespoons sugar
- ¼ teaspoon salt
- 9 tablespoons (1 stick plus 1 tablespoon) unsalted butter, frozen and cut into bits
- 1 egg yolk
- 1½ tablespoons cold water

FILLING

- 10 ripe red plums
- ¼ cup freshly squeezed lemon juice
- 2 tablespoons sugar
- 3 tablespoons honey
- 1 cup whipped cream

To make the crust, mix dry ingredients using a food processor. Add butter and process just until mixture resembles coarse cornmeal. Mix the egg yolk and water, then add to the bowl of the food processor with motor running and process just until the dough almost forms a ball. Refrigerate until ready to use.

Preheat the oven to 400 degrees. To make the filling, drop the plums in boiling water for about a minute to make peeling easier and then use a paring knife. Cut each in half and remove pit. Place plums in a bowl with the lemon juice, coating well.

Remove dough from refrigerator. On a floured surface, roll out to fit into an 11-inch rectangular tart pan with a removable bottom. Arrange plums neatly in rows on the pastry, then sprinkle with the sugar. Bake for 25 to 30 minutes, until pastry has turned golden and plums are tender. Let cool thoroughly. Remove tart from pan. Warm the honey and glaze each plum. Fill between the rows with whipped cream.

Serves 8 to 10

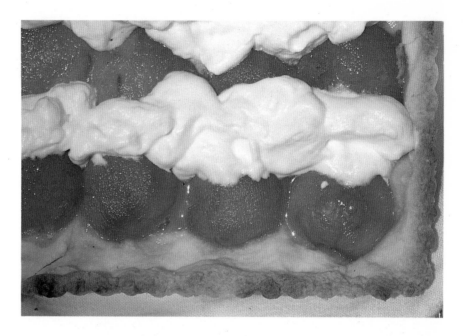

CLARA NELL ADAMS WHITE CHOCOLATE CAKE

C. N. Adams was famous for this cake. You'll taste why.

CAKE

- 1 cup (2 sticks) unsalted butter, softened
- 1½ cups sugar
- 4 eggs, separated
- ⅓ cup grated white chocolate
- ½ cup water
- 2½ cups all-purpose flour
- 1 teaspoon baking soda
- 1 cup buttermilk
- 1 teaspoon vanilla extract

ICING

- ½ cup plus 2 tablespoons sugar
- ¾ cup evaporated milk
- 4 tablespoons (½ stick) unsalted butter
- 1 teaspoon vanilla extract
- 2 cups grated white chocolate

Preheat the oven to 350 degrees. Grease and lightly flour three 9-inch round cake pans.

To make the cake, cream the butter and sugar until light and fluffy. Beat in the egg yolks, one at a time. Set aside.

Combine the white chocolate and water in a small saucepan over low heat. Carefully melt (be sure not to let it scorch) and beat into the butter mixture. Sift together the flour and baking soda. Add to the creamed mixture, alternating with the buttermilk. Stir in vanilla. Beat egg whites until stiff, then fold into the batter.

Divide batter equally among the 3 pans and bake for 20 minutes, or until a cake tester comes out clean and layers are turning golden. Let rest a few minutes before loosening edges and inverting onto cooling racks. When cool, brush off crumbs.

To make icing, combine sugar, evaporated milk, and butter in a saucepan over low heat. When the butter has melted, lightly boil for 1 minute. Stir in vanilla. Off the heat, beat in the white chocolate until it is completely melted. Let cool to a spreadable consistency.

Serves 10 to 12

LEMON-BLUEBERRY TARTLETS

You will like this lemony pastry.

- 3 tablespoons sugar
- 2⅓ cups all-purpose flour
- ¾ teaspoon salt
- ⅔ cup unsalted butter, chilled and cut into bits
- 2 tablespoons freshly squeezed lemon juice
- 3 tablespoons ice water
- 1 pint blueberries, washed
- 2 tablespoons honey
- 1 tablespoon freshly grated lemon rind
- Whipped cream (optional)

Combine the sugar, flour, and salt in a food processor and pulse several times to mix. Add the butter and process until mixture is the texture of coarse meal. Add lemon juice and water, and process until dough begins to form a ball. Gather into a ball, flatten slightly between sheets of waxed paper, and refrigerate for 1 hour.

Preheat the oven to 400 degrees. Roll out dough to about ¼-inch thick and cut into 5-inch circles. (Use a coffee or shortening can to cut these circles.) Line 12 large muffin cups with the dough, then prick the bottoms and sides with the tines of a fork. Bake for 15 minutes, or until golden. Check several times for the air bubbles that can form as the dough bakes and pierce them with the point of a knife as they appear. Cool partially in the pan, then carefully lift out.

Combine berries, honey, and lemon rind, then use to fill each cup. Top with a dab of whipped cream, if you like.

Makes 12 tarts

LAYERED BOURBON ICE BOX CAKE

Here is a Southern trifle.

- 6 egg yolks
- ⅔ cup sugar
- ¾ cup bourbon
- ½ teaspoon grated nutmeg
- ½ teaspoon ground cinnamon
- ⅛ teaspoon ground allspice
- 1 plain loaf pound-cake, in ½-inch slices

Whip together the yolks and sugar in the top of a double boiler. Stir in the bourbon and spices. Cook over lightly boiling water, stirring constantly, for 5 minutes until thick and custardlike. Press a sheet of waxed paper onto the top and allow to cool.

When custard is cool, assemble cake by layering cake slices and custard in a glass bowl, ending with the custard. Cover and refrigerate for half a day before serving.

This will keep very well for several days.

Serves 8 to 12

LEMON SAND TARTS

These are perfect to serve with ice cream or iced tea.

- 1¼ cups sugar
- ¾ cup (1½ sticks) unsalted butter, softened
- 1 egg plus 1 egg yolk
- ½ teaspoon vanilla extract
- 2 teaspoons freshly squeezed lemon juice
- 1 teaspoon freshly grated lemon rind
- 3 cups all-purpose flour
- ¼ teaspoon salt
- Sugar for sprinkling

Cream the sugar and butter until light and fluffy. Beat in the egg and egg yolk, then stir in vanilla, lemon juice, and rind. Beat in flour and salt to form a stiff dough. Gather into a ball and flatten between sheets of waxed paper. Refrigerate for 1 hour.

Preheat the oven to 400 degrees. Grease 2 baking sheets. Roll dough until thin, cut into 2-inch rounds, and sprinkle rounds, with additional sugar. Place on baking sheets and bake for 9 minutes, or until just beginning to turn golden.

Makes approximately 50

CHOCOLATE CHIP– PEANUT BUTTER– WALNUT COOKIES

This is obviously one of those "anything goes" cookies. You might want to substitute another nut for the walnuts and change the chocolate chips to white or dark chocolate chunks— or use a combination of several kinds.

- 1 cup (2 sticks) unsalted butter, softened
- ¾ cup firmly packed dark brown sugar
- ¾ cup granulated sugar
- 1 teaspoon vanilla extract
- ½ teaspoon water
- 2 eggs
- 2 cups all-purpose flour
- 1 teaspoon baking soda
- 1 teaspoon salt
- 1 cup coarsely chopped walnuts
- 1 cup semisweet chocolate chips
- 1 cup peanut butter chips

Preheat the oven to 375 degrees. Grease a baking sheet. Cream together the butter, sugars, vanilla, and water until fluffy. Beat in eggs one at a time. Sift the flour, soda, and salt together. Blend into the creamed mixture. Fold in nuts and chips. Drop by tablespoonsful onto baking sheet and bake about 10 minutes, until lightly browned.

Makes approximately 60

NATCHEZ LEMON CAKE

An old cake recipe, wonderfully moist and tart—and like most old Southern dessert recipes, very sweet.

CAKE

- ⅔ cup unsalted butter, or half butter and half margarine, softened
- 1½ cups sugar
- 2 tablespoons freshly grated lemon peel
- 2½ teaspoons freshly squeezed lemon juice
- 4 eggs
- 2 cups plus 3 tablespoons all-purpose flour
- 2½ teaspoons baking powder
- ¼ teaspoon salt
- ¾ cup milk

LEMON FILLING

- 1½ cups sugar
- ¼ cup cornstarch
  Pinch of salt
- 1 cup water
- 6 tablespoons freshly squeezed lemon juice
- 4 teaspoons freshly grated lemon peel
- 2 tablespoons unsalted butter
- 6 egg yolks, lightly beaten
  Whipped cream (optional)
  Berry purée (optional)

Preheat the oven to 375 degrees. Grease and flour three 9-inch round cake pans. Set aside.

To make the cake, cream the butter and sugar until light and fluffy. Add the lemon peel and juice, then add eggs, one at a time, mixing well after each.

Sift the flour with the baking powder and salt. Add to batter, alternating with the milk and beginning and ending with the flour.

Pour batter into prepared pans.

Bake, being careful not to let pans touch one another, for 20 minutes, or until a cake tester comes out clean. Allow to cool slightly in the pan, then loosen edges and invert cakes onto cooling racks. When completely cooled, dust crumbs off layers.

To make the filling, sift the sugar, cornstarch, and salt into the top of a double boiler. Stir in the water, lemon juice, and peel. Add the butter and cook, stirring, for 6 minutes. Cover and cook another 10 minutes without stirring. Remove from the heat and stir in the yolks. Return to heat and cook about 3 minutes, until mixture begins to coat spoon. If any globs of egg yolk have solidified in the mixture, pick them out. Cool for 45 minutes, stirring occasionally.

To assemble, place 1 layer on a cake plate with the bottom side up and spoon on some of the filling a little at a time so it will be absorbed, continuing until it starts to run off. Hold the second layer in one hand, bottom side up, and spoon filling over it, allowing it to soak in as with the first layer. Carefully turn it over and position on top of the first layer, wet side down. Spoon more filling on top. (Filling will not be absorbed as readily as it was on the undersides.) Prepare the top layer as you did the second, bottom side up, then turn it over and place on top of second layer. Spoon remaining filling over top layer and allow to run down sides.

This filling is very liquid and takes a while to set. Serve cake with whipped cream or a berry purée.

Serves 12 to 14

AUNT LADY CARTER'S ANGEL PIE

This is a delicious, light pie.

- 3 egg whites
- ½ cup granulated sugar
- ⅓ cup confectioners' sugar
- 1 cup heavy cream
- 1 ounce or more semisweet or sweet chocolate

Preheat the oven to 300 degrees. Beat the egg whites until stiff but not dry. Beat in granulated sugar, then fold in confectioners' sugar. Pour batter into an ungreased 9-inch pie pan and bake for 1 hour. This will puff up and be lightly golden, like ordinary meringue.

Allow to cool.

About 2 hours before serving, whip the cream. Crush the top of the meringue if it has not already settled, and fill crust with the cream. Grate the chocolate over the top. Refrigerate until ready to serve.

Serves 6 to 8

CAFÉ AU LAIT ICE CREAM

This is another recipe for using leftovers, this time breakfast coffee. Make sure you use a strong cup of coffee.

- ½ cup sugar
- ¾ cup milk, scalded
- 2 egg yolks
- ¾ cup heavy cream
- 1 cup strong French roast coffee

Heat the sugar in a heavy skillet over very low heat for 30 minutes, stirring constantly until sugar is melted and light brown. Remove from heat and pour in scalded milk, which will foam and steam briefly. Return to low heat and stir for 5 minutes, until all the caramel melts.

In a large bowl, beat the egg yolks until light and add the hot milk mixture slowly, stirring. Return it to skillet and cook over very low heat for 10 minutes, until thickened. Allow to cool before adding the cream and coffee. Refrigerate until cold and then freeze in an ice-cream freezer following the manufacturer's instructions.

Makes 1 pint

OPPOSITE ABOVE: **Aunt Lady Carter's Angel Pie.** OPPOSITE BELOW: **Natchez Lemon Cake.** BELOW: **Café au Lait Ice Cream.** BOTTOM: **Bread Pudding Ice Cream.**

BREAD PUDDING ICE CREAM

Bread pudding is a very popular dessert here, as it is throughout the Deep South. This ice cream recipe was probably just a handy way to utilize leftover bread pudding.

- 2 eggs
- ⅔ cup sugar
- 1⅓ cups milk
- 2 cups heavy cream
- 2 teaspoons vanilla extract or bourbon
- 1 cup cubed bread pudding (½-inch cubes)

Beat eggs and sugar together for 5 minutes, until thick and creamy. Stir in milk, cream, and vanilla or bourbon. Refrigerate overnight. Freeze in an ice-cream freezer following the manufacturer's instructions. Halfway through the process, add bread pudding cubes and finish.

Makes about 1 quart

Index

-mustard dressing, melon and grape
salad with, 66
tomatoes, baked, 32
hot-water corn bread, 93
hunter's sauce, 130

I

ice cream:
bourbon-mint, 42
bread pudding, 173
café au lait, 173
fig preserves, 112
see also sherbet
iced beet and orange soup, 55

K

kiss rolls, 73

L

layered bourbon ice box cake, 170
lemon:
-blueberry tartlets, 170
cake, Natchez, 172
carrots, 119
-pineapple mousse, 144
sand tarts, 171

M

mayonnaise, 101
tomato aspic with, 20
melon:
with blueberry sauce, 83
and grape salad with honey-mustard
dressing, 66
meringue and peach "shortcake," 105
mint-bourbon ice cream, 42
mousse, pineapple-lemon, 144
mushroom(s):
buttered rice and, 41
consommé, 157
mustard greens with pepper vinegar, 40

N

Natchez:
lemon cake, 172
seafood salad, 80–81
Sloe Gin Rickey, 30
new potatoes and string beans, 96

O

okra:
pickled, 103
pilaf, 88
onion(s):
caramelized, 136
glazed carrots, turnips and, 151
green, spring peas and, 20
sautéed, 39
tart, 127
yellow squash and, 97

orange and beet soup, iced, 55
oyster(s):
and corn chowder, 163
poached spinach-wrapped, 157

P

pan-sautéed catfish fillets with parsley-
pecan sauce, 118
parsley:
butter, 88
-pecan sauce, 118
peach(es):
-and-cream cake, 97
and meringue "shortcake," 105
sherbet, 58
peanut butter-chocolate chip-walnut
cookies, 171
pear-almond torte, 166
pecan:
-cinnamon squares, 153
-parsley sauce, 118
rice, 22
pickled okra, 103
pickles, watermelon rind, 144
pie:
Aunt Lady Carter's angel, 172
chess, with blackberry sauce, 123
deep dish dewberry, with cream, 49
deep dish ham and eggplant, 102
gumbo, with salt corn bread crust, 142
pilaf, okra, 88
pineapple-lemon mousse, 144
plum:
jam cake with rum whipped cream, 67
tart, 169
poached spinach-wrapped oysters, 157
popovers, 151
pork, roast loin of, with natural
gravy, 165
potato(es):
new, string beans and, 96
scalloped, 127
see also sweet potato(es)
preserves, Freddie's fig, 112
purée of beets and carrots, 73

Q

quail, smothered, 109

R

rice:
buttered, mushrooms and, 41
dirty, 158
pecan, 22
wild, with peppers, 149
yellow, 57
roast loin of pork with natural gravy, 165
roast venison with hunter's sauce, 130
rosemary string beans, 65
rum:
-butter shrimp, 56

whipped cream, plum jam cake
with, 67

S

salad:
black-eyed pea, with champagne
vinaigrette, 33
chopped, with pepper mayonnaise, 101
green pea and dill, 143
melon and grape, with honey-mustard
dressing, 66
Natchez seafood, 80–81
summer garden, 87
salt corn bread crust, 142
sauerkraut, wild ducks baked in, with
duck-leg gravy, 150
sausage, spring, with sautéed
onions, 39
sautéed onions, 39
scalloped potatoes, 127
seafood salad, Natchez, 80–81
sherbet:
berry, 74
peach, 58
sherry spice cake with brown sugar glaze,
159
shrimp:
butter-rum, 56
tarragon creamed river chicken
and, 63
skillet:
asparagus, 47
corn bread, 41
fresh corn, 34
slaw, buttered steamed, 110
Sloe Gin Rickey, Natchez, 30
slow oven-barbecued brisket, 32
smothered crawfish with ham stuffing, 48
smothered quail, 109
soup:
acorn squash, 149
carrot and sweet red pepper, 80
corn and oyster chowder, 163
iced beet and orange, 55
spiced sweet potatoes, 164
spicy milk fried chicken with pan
gravy, 23
spinach:
creamy, 165
-wrapped oysters, poached, 157
spring peas and green onions, 20
spring sausage with sautéed onions, 39
squash:
buttered acorn, 159
soufflé, yellow, with fresh tomato and
sweet red pepper sauce, 117
soup, acorn, 149
yellow, and onions, 97
steamed:
broccoli and cauliflower, 136
caraway cucumbers, 72
stewed tomatoes, 96
strawberries with brown sugar and sour
cream, 35

string beans:
    new potatoes and, 96
    rosemary, 65
sugar cookies, 43
summer garden salad, 87
sweet potato(es):
    biscuits, 131
    chips, 136
    spiced, 164
sweet red pepper:
    and carrot soup, 80
    and fresh tomato sauce, 117

T

Tabasco butter, 82
tarragon creamed river shrimp and
    chicken, 63

tomato(es):
    aspic with mayonnaise, 20
    baked honey, 32
    fresh, and sweet red pepper sauce, 117
    stewed, 96
turnip greens, 96
turnips, glazed carrots, onions and, 151

V

venison, roast, with hunter's sauce, 130
vinegar, pepper, mustard greens with, 40

W

walnut:
    -blackberry conserve, 111
    -chocolate chip-peanut butter cookies,
    171

warm applesauce with cream, 152
warm curried fruit, 74
watermelon rind pickles, 144
wild ducks baked in sauerkraut, with
    duck-leg gravy, 150
wild rice with peppers, 149

Y

yellow rice, 57
yellow squash and onions, 97
yellow squash soufflé with fresh tomato
    and sweet red pepper sauce, 117

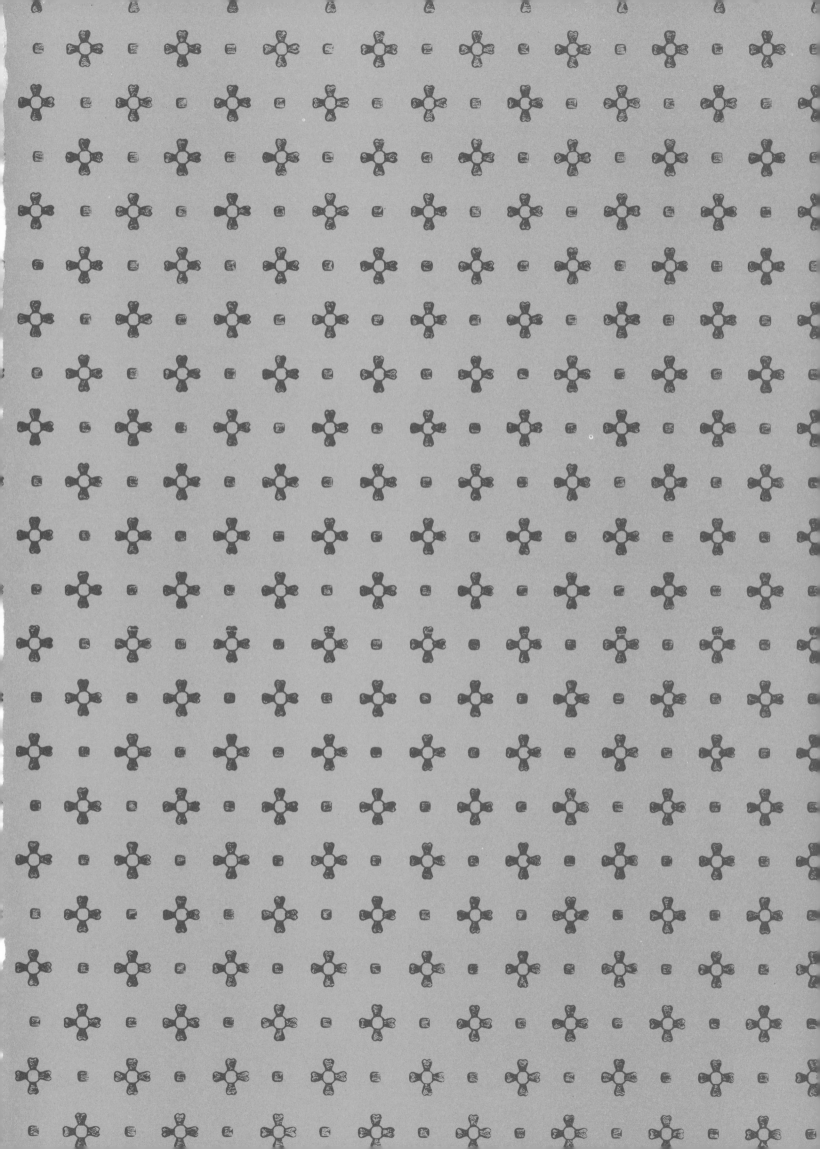